ALAN TITCHMARSH
LOVE YOUR
GARDEN

EBURY
PRESS

10 9 8 7 6 5 4 3 2 1

Published in 2012 by Ebury Press, an imprint of Ebury Publishing
a Random House Group Company

Text copyright © Granada Ventures Limited trading ITV Studios Global
Entertainment.
All images copyright © Spun Gold TV Limited apart from Jonathan
Buckley: cover, 4, 6, 72, 86, 130, 144, 152; Derek St Romaine Garden
Photo Library: 22, 31, 37, 78, 102, 151, 160; Getty Images: cover, 37,
40, 56, 95, 114, 117, 126, 136, 176
Garden plan illustrations © Mat Johnstone 2012
Illustrations © Hayley Merrington 2012

The television series *Love Your Garden* is a Spun Gold TV Limited
production for ITV

The Random House Group Limited Reg. No. 954009

Addresses for companies within the Random House Group can
be found at www.randomhouse.co.uk

A CIP catalogue record for this book is available from the British Library

The Random House Group Limited supports The Forest Stewardship
Council (FSC®), the leading international forest certification
organisation. Our books carrying the FSC label are printed on
FSC® certified paper. FSC is the only forest certification scheme
endorsed by the leading environmental organisations, including
Greenpeace. Our paper procurement policy can be found at
www.randomhouse.co.uk/environment

To buy books by your favourite authors and register for offers
visit www.randomhouse.co.uk

Design: Smith & Gilmour, London
Picture researcher: Victoria Hall

Printed and bound by Butler Tanner and Dennis Ltd, Frome

ISBN 9780091948665

CONTENTS

INTRODUCTION

Deep down in our subconscious, we all have a dream garden waiting to break out. Yours might be a secret retreat where you can escape from the world, or perhaps you pine for a chic, city-centre bachelor pad. Maybe you'd love a romantic rose-laden haven, a private wildlife sanctuary or a luxurious personal spa. Perhaps your taste leans towards a beach-hut get-away by the sea, surrounded by coastal plants and nautical knick knacks, or a country cottage garden packed with fragrant flowers and edible plants.

Whatever your garden fantasy, it can be turned into reality. No, you don't need a lottery win, and you can manage perfectly well without stately acres or the services of a top garden designer. With a little effort even the smallest patch of ground can be transformed into a stylish garden – a pocket-hanky-size patch actually gives far more scope for a 'make-over' than a big garden, since you can allocate more time and money per square foot. Less is more when it comes to packing a designer punch as you can concentrate on creating one particular idea and developing the theme to the full. Long narrow plots, which are commonly found behind urban properties, also have bags of potential as they divide up easily into a series of interconnecting 'rooms', so don't feel they present a disadvantage – quite the reverse. In a small space you can really go for it.

Over the next twelve chapters I'll show you how to create a dozen of the most popular themes that recur in people's fantasy gardens. And besides the plants and the hardware that it takes to bring each particular 'theme' to life, I'll be looking at the other spin offs that branch out as you develop a particular interest – whether it's outdoor arts and crafts, recipes, wildlife, outdoor entertaining or self-sufficiency.

All it takes are the right techniques, plants, accessories and design tips for putting a garden together successfully. Then just add time, attention and, the magic ingredient, love. It might sound silly, but love sure as heck makes a great garden. It's the best fertiliser you'll meet, and you can't bottle it – it has to come from the heart. So go ahead, unlock your garden's hidden potential. It can change your life.

CHAPTER I

THE TRADITIONAL BRITISH GARDEN

A staggering eight out of ten people in Britain live on the outskirts of towns and cities, so suburban gardens are the type we all see most of. The classic suburban garden might sound very ordinary and even a bit middle class, making you think of the gardens of your youth – well, mine anyway – all very 'proper' with tightly pruned rose beds, closely mown lawns, neat rows of bedding plants and peep-proof hedges. But behind lots of otherwise ordinary-looking homes there are some extraordinary gardens, with even the smallest plots transformed into spectacular dream spaces. Anyone can do it – all it takes is a bit of time and effort. You don't even need to spend a fortune.

Combine hard landscaping (paths and fences, buildings and sculpture) with foliage and flowers to create an atmosphere that is both comforting and restful.

WHAT MAKES A TRADITIONAL BRITISH GARDEN?

The essence of a traditional garden is traditional ingredients. There'll be a lush, well-cared-for lawn flanked by closely planted borders designed to create as much colour and interest as possible for most of the year. You'll find hedges or fencing around the boundaries to provide privacy. It'll usually contain a bit of everything that the owners are interested in – roses, shrubs and perennial flowers, a bit of paving with tubs and hanging baskets, water and a fruit and veg patch. There's also likely to be a summerhouse for relaxing in, plants and habitats for wildlife, and safe places for children and pets to play. The ideal traditional garden marries a blend of creativity (the artistic side), cultivation (the hard work bit) and relaxation (sitting down and enjoying it), so it's vital to keep the balance just right.

Top tip: material choices

Use matching materials or colours all around your garden to 'pull everything together', particularly when you're planning a complicated scheme. Paint all the wood the same colour (arches, summerhouses, plant supports and obelisks, etc), use the same kind of paving for paths and patios and use complementary edging around the lawn.

GET THE LOOK

THE DESIGN

Seamless design allows a garden to flow effortlessly from one area to the next, making the space look much bigger than it really is. The trick is to work the design so you can't see your entire garden from the house. This will encourage you – literally up the garden path – to wander round and discover everything as you go.

Instead of having the usual rectangular lawn outlined with narrow beds, be bold. Create a set of generously-sized 'feature beds' flanking the lawn, with curved sinuous shapes that make for a showy effect. If you need inspiration, divide a square or rectangular plot up into interesting shapes by using a figure-of-eight-shaped lawn arranged at an angle from corner to corner in your plot, with the largest 'half' closest to the house.

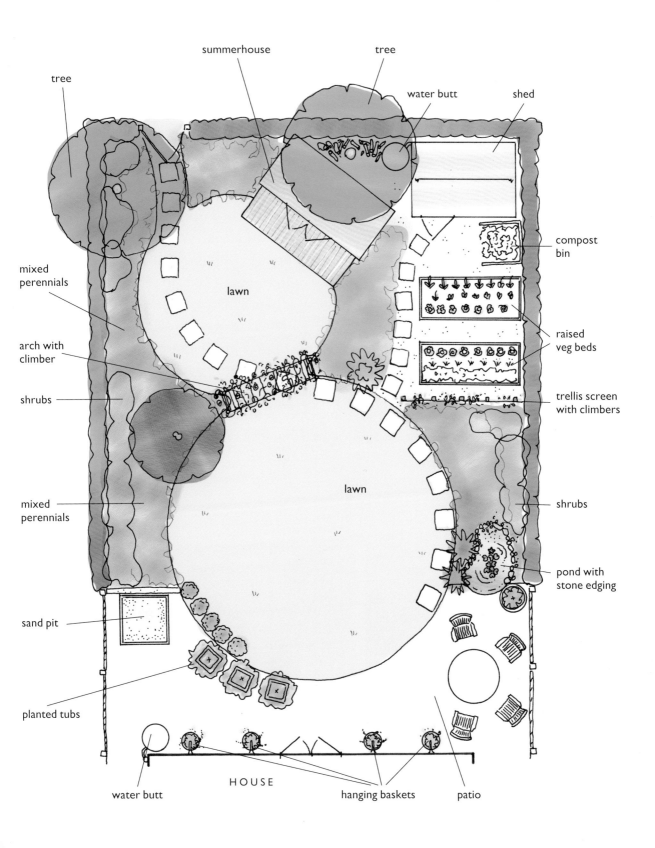

tree

summerhouse

tree

water butt

shed

mixed
perennials

compost
bin

arch with
climber

lawn

raised
veg beds

shrubs

trellis screen
with climbers

mixed
perennials

lawn

shrubs

sand pit

pond with
stone edging

planted tubs

water butt

hanging baskets

patio

H O U S E

The narrow gap where the two circles meet in the middle automatically makes an entrance into a different area of the garden, perhaps with an arch over the top or a paved step to underline the change of scene.

Be practical and make sure you've planned for all the things you actually need in the garden. A paved area close to the house is handy for sitting outside in summer and also provides a good setting for tubs and hanging baskets as you can see them well from indoors. Don't forget to include 'working' areas in your design, as most gardens need space for compost bins, a tool shed and dustbins. Also make sure garden paths lead to the shed, back gate and other places you'll need to go. Allow space for drying laundry – a rotary airer doesn't take up much room but needs a 'socket' to sit in and an area of short grass, gravel or paving underneath. Alternatively, place it in the centre of a circle of gravel planted with low creeping thymes to double as a fragrant herb garden when not in use – as a bonus it scents the laundry hanging above it on wash-days. Veggie beds are usually banished to the far end of the garden as they don't always look great. However, if space is short make a decorative potager-style edible area that looks as good as a flower garden.

Top tip: lawn edging

Bricks make an economical and good-looking lawn edge, but for a period look use Victorian-style rope-topped edging tiles in blue-grey or terracotta. If your budget is tight, opt for quick-to-install plastic edging strip. It is hardwearing and makes a largely maintenance-free finish. Sink it into the soil so the top is level with the base of the turf, and you can simply push the mower over the top, which saves a lot of hand-clipping with shears to neaten lawn edges after mowing.

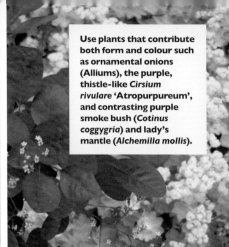

Use plants that contribute both form and colour such as ornamental onions (Alliums), the purple, thistle-like *Cirsium rivulare* 'Atropurpureum', and contrasting purple smoke bush (*Cotinus coggygria*) and lady's mantle (*Alchemilla mollis*).

THE PLANTS

A traditional garden needs **generous planting** so you see little or no bare soil between the plants. Match the plants to the growing conditions in your garden, and measure your borders carefully so you can work out exactly how many plants to buy (eventual plant sizes are given on the label). If you have room for six plants don't get six completely different sorts – buy three of two types as this will provide more impact.

When space is tight, **choose plants that look good for much of the year**, perhaps with several separate 'best' seasons. Japanese maples are a good example, with elegant ferny foliage that turns fiery red in autumn, then drops to leave a handsome skeleton shape that stands out well in winter – what's more they won't outgrow a small garden. Crab apples have great spring blossom followed by colourful fruit in autumn. And **clipped topiary** shapes look good all year round, and are great for showing off seasonal flowers.

Choose groups of plants that need the **same growing conditions**. For shade, hosta, hardy ferns and Japanese maple is a winning combination. Purple smoke bush (*Cotinus coggygria*) and bright green, frothy-textured lady's mantle is another. For sun, try roses and lamb's ears (*Stachys byzantina*), lavender and purple fennel, or ice plant (*Sedum spectabile*) with reddish-tinged carex sedge. When space is short try two different varieties of creeping lysimachia in pale gold and purple – a duo which is good for a pot if there's no room on the ground.

A STAR FEATURE

Every traditional garden needs a star feature to act as a focal point and catch your eye. A summerhouse does the job brilliantly, while also providing somewhere for you to relax and store a barbecue and garden furniture.

If you are good with your hands, you could save money by building your own summerhouse out of recycled materials. Don't worry if DIY isn't your thing, as it's easy to customise a traditional pressure-treated timber building with coloured preservative. If money is no object you might go for a contemporary outdoor 'pod' that rotates so you can follow the sun during the day. Whatever, a bit of decking outside the door increases the seating space, and gives a tiny building more emphasis. A crafty way to double-up on the interest is to combine the summerhouse and decking with a pond. To make maximum use of limited space run the decking out over part of the water, which looks spectacular (almost gravity-defying) and gives you two uses in the space of one.

Dig a new bed

Don't try to dig out beds free-hand. 'Draw' them on the ground before digging – this also gives you the opportunity to see the shape from various angles and judge the effect before committing yourself.

1. Use a hosepipe to outline the shape of your new bed. Leave it out in the sun (or run hot water through it in cold weather) to make it soft and pliable. Lay it out on the lawn to create a flowing sinuous shape with gentle curves – it's easily altered until you are happy with the result.

2. Use kiln-dried sand (which is very fine and bone-dry so it trickles easily); funnel it in an old wine bottle then use this to trickle sand round the edge of the hose where you want the bed.

3. Take the hose away then get the spade and start cutting out the outline of your bed. Strip off the turf, and dig the soil over. Work in plenty of well-rotted organic matter, and some general fertiliser such as blood, fish and bone meal to improve growing conditions, then you're ready to start planting.

Top tip: buying plants

Stand plants together in the garden centre when you're buying. This will give you an idea if they work well as a group and how they'll look in your garden. Also check their expected size to be sure you have enough room for them at home.

Create a natural pond edge

Ponds are made or marred by their edges. Rocks, moisture-loving plants and water make natural partners, but lots of people go wrong by dotting blob-shaped rocks around randomly between the wrong sort of plants, which looks most unnatural. Another common water-gardening mistake is to mound soil up round a pond so every time it rains there's nothing to stop it being washed down into the water, where the nutrients feed microscopic algae – which is why the water turns green.

The solution is to make a stone edging around the pond and plant adjacent to it so that foliage tumbles attractively over the stones towards the water. This creates a natural look that also acts as an effective barrier. You can create an edging like this round a new pond when you've first made it, or alter an existing pond edge so it all looks – and works – better later.

1. Clear everything from the edge of the pond so you have a space in which to start work. Choose stones with some flat sides and place them right along the edge of the water so they overhang a bit. Bed them down onto a thin layer of compost to cushion the pond liner and avoid puncturing it. Use aquatic compost or poorish garden topsoil taken from a place that hasn't had fertiliser used for some time – don't use highly fertile soil or potting compost since it's too rich and the nutrients will turn the water green.

2. Add more compost behind the stones to create a damp bed for moisture-loving pondside plants. Hostas and astilbes are superb, as they have colour, good foliage and great textures and shapes. Use good-sized plants so you get an instant effect, and plant them so they fall naturally down towards the water.

3. Spread a layer of smooth, rounded, golf-ball-sized pebbles over the soil between the plants and stone edging. This creates a natural-looking mulch that sets off the foliage and seals moisture into the soil, maintaining the boggy conditions the plants enjoy. The pebbles and stones will also help prevent rain from washing loose soil into the pond – any that escapes will be trapped by the edging of stones so it can't fall into the pond and foul the water.

Making a jetty

1. Construct your jetty at the same time as your pond to prevent the pond liner being perforated by the weight-bearing posts.

2. Sit half a concrete block underneath the liner where the posts will go and cushion it with an old piece of carpet. (fig. 1)

3. Complete the pond and fit the liner, then feel where the concrete blocks sit and lay another piece of carpet over the top (above the liner this time).

4. Sit another half block on top of the carpet. This well-cushioned block-and-carpet sandwich will support the weight of a jetty post with no risk of piercing the liner. (fig. 2)

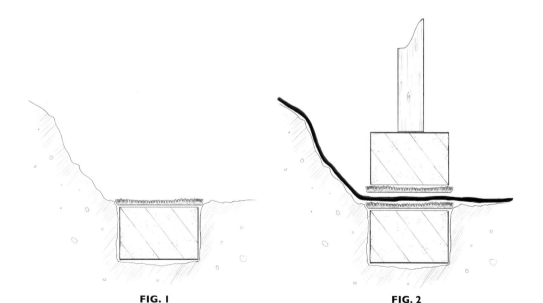

FIG. 1   **FIG. 2**

Top tip: native pond plants

Healthy ponds need lots of oxygenating plants. The kind that's easily available and often recommended for the job is Canadian pondweed, but it's far too rampant for a small pond – it'll often take over completely within its first year. You're far better off choosing British native water plants like hornwort or water milfoil which have frothy ferny foliage and aren't half so vigorous. Ask for them in the water section at garden centres, or visit a specialist aquatic centre.

GARDENING WITH CATS

Increasingly all sorts of wildlife are finding that urban and suburban surroundings provide richer pickings than the countryside, where suitable habitat is declining. But in gardens, wild creatures have to contend with a problem they don't meet so much out of town – pets. A recent study showed that Britain's 10.3 million cats kill over 160 million small creatures each year. That includes a good many mice, rats and voles (which you probably aren't so keen on encouraging into your garden) along with a great deal of birds. The challenge for suburban gardeners is to create conditions that allow wildlife to visit in safety, without risk from our feline predators. Here are a few solutions:

Catatorium It's like an aviary, but with the birds on the outside. Cover a short pergola all over with fruit cage netting – sides and top – which the cat or cats go inside. It looks good as it can be planted as usual with climbers, etc; put a weatherproof 'house' inside if you leave cats out while you're at work – as a bonus, it means pets stay safe from traffic. Meanwhile birds can use the garden in safety – they'll come right up to the netting as they know they are safe.

Pelleted lion poo This is sold especially for deterring cats and is meant to fool intruding moggies into thinking a bigger, stronger predator is in residence. Sadly it didn't deter our test cat.

Sonic sensors An electronic device run by batteries, or from the mains, that sets off a loud, high-pitched noise at a frequency only cats can hear. It is triggered by movement at cat-height. Many people find them very effective (especially the mains-powered version, as the gadget simply stops working if the battery runs out and you have no way of telling till cats start coming back).

Bells A tinkling cat collar gives birds early warning, and works quite well – but your neighbour's cats may not have bells, so don't assume birds are entirely safe.

Safe environment Create safe feeding places, by hanging bird feeders up high and positioning bird tables in the open but with trees and bushes within easy access so birds can see trouble coming and escape. Use birdbaths on plinths, as they give a better field of view than water at ground level, and put 'cat guards' round the base of bird tables so cats can't climb up.

MAKE THE MOST OF A TRADITIONAL BRITISH GARDEN – KEEP BEES

That most genteel British pastime, bee-keeping, has spread its wings. It's no longer solely practised by country gardeners and today some of the most productive hives are in towns, cities and suburbs where garden flowers provide good sources of nectar. A single WBC beehive (the standard sort with a series of overlapping tiers holding the honey chambers and a pitch roof over the top, standing on short legs) can produce forty pounds of honey per year, and takes up very little space.

A hive of bees isn't dangerous, though clearly the inhabitants are capable of administering some painful stings if they feel the need to defend themselves, so take advice from local beekeepers about siting and caring for a hive – they'll also be able to put you in touch with suppliers of bees, hives, a set of bee-proof protective coveralls and other basic equipment such as a smoker (a few puffs of smoke up the entrance slot at the base of the hive calms bees down so you can open the hive to inspect progress or remove honey). Find information and details of local groups from the British Beekeepers Association (www.bbka.org.uk).

Besides the annual honey harvest in autumn, bees do a great job of pollinating flower, which is especially important for anyone who grows fruit and veggies. It's also very relaxing to watch them at work while you're out enjoying your garden – the background buzzing is very peaceful and 'blanks out' the usual traffic noises in an urban environment.

Bees are indeed busy; it takes *a couple of million trips* to produce one pound of honey. They start work early in spring as soon as there are flowers opening, so it pays to keep the garden well stocked with late winter and early spring blooms as well as the more familiar summer sort. In winter most of the worker bees die off, leaving just the queen and a few attendants.

HONEY ICE CREAM

SERVES: 4–6

Preparation time:
45 minutes
(3 hours if you don't
have an ice-cream maker)

Ingredients
250ml full-fat milk
570ml double cream
10 large free-range
   egg yolks
110g runny honey

Method

1. Pour the milk and cream into a saucepan, heat gently and bring to the boil.

2. Remove the pan from the heat as soon as the mixture boils.

3. Put the egg yolks into a bowl and add the honey; whisk together until the mixture is pale and creamy.

4. Pour the hot milk and cream onto the eggs-and-honey mixture, whisking continuously until the mixture is smooth and well combined.

5. Return the mixture to a clean saucepan and warm over a low heat, stirring continuously until the mixture is thick enough to coat the back of a spoon.

6. Remove the saucepan from the heat and transfer the mixture to a clean bowl, cover with cling film and leave to cool.

If using an ice-cream maker:

Pour the cooled mixture into a pre-frozen ice-cream maker bowl and churn according to the manufacturer's instructions until thick and smooth.

If making by hand:

1. Pour the cooled mixture into a freezer-proof bowl and place in the freezer.

2. Remove the mixture every two hours, stir vigorously and put back into the freezer. Do this until the mixture has set.

CHAPTER 2

THE COUNTRY GARDEN

Centuries ago, most of the British population lived in the countryside and their gardens were all about self-sufficiency; they acted as part living larder, part smallholding and part herbal pharmacy. Today's country gardens look back on this legacy in the wealth of colourful flowers and plants that we grow, many of which originally had useful functions that we've largely forgotten – now we simply grow them for their good looks and rural ambience. And although the picture that springs to mind of a 'typical' country garden today has more in common with chocolate boxes than real-life, you can still create the timeless qualities of a romantic rural retreat – even if you live on a housing estate – by using fragrant old-fashioned flowers and rustic features.

Country gardens are typified by the use of old bricks as paving material, rusted metal structures, clay flowerpots and the use of billowing banks of flowers in apparent disarray.

WHAT MAKES A COUNTRY GARDEN?

The heart and soul of a country garden is flowers, and lots of them, growing apparently randomly to create a patchwork-quilt effect. Beds are a riot of colour created by blending old-fashioned perennials, hardy annuals and plants that were once used as medicinal or cosmetic herbs. There'll often be a few formal touches to bring a slight sense of order to the chaos – perhaps dwarf box edging along a path to hold back the flowers, or a few pieces of topiary. But every scrap of space is used, from fruit trees grown flat against sunny walls to pumpkins growing on top of the compost heap. There's also lots of detail – containers, winding paths, structures and outdoor arts and crafts – used to create contrasts and extra space for plants. And even in small gardens, the space is often cunningly divided up to create a series of 'garden rooms', each with its own character, so the centre of interest is constantly changing through the seasons. These are gardens for people who love plants and pottering.

GET THE LOOK

THE DESIGN

A country garden is by nature a bit rambling. It starts at the house with an area of stone-flagged terrace leading down to lawns enclosed by generous borders backed by hedges or rustic poles for climbers. There may be smaller, irregular-shaped island beds set within the grass. Traditionally there'd be a large apple or plum tree in the lawn, often with spring bulbs naturalised in rough grass underneath. Winding gravel or stone-paved paths encourage people to wander around – they may lead under a rose-clad pergola or perhaps down to the kitchen garden and hen run. Or they may lead to a summerhouse, fishpond or a wild area left to nature beyond. It sounds huge, but trust me – it can all be scaled down quite successfully. It's the atmosphere you are trying to recreate.

Top tip: edging paths

In country gardens it's traditional to use a row of plants to edge paths or flower-beds – the foliage 'softens' the straight edges. Here are my favourite options:

♣ Small compact perennials such as lady's mantle or variegated brunnera are good grown as informal edgings that spill softly over grass, gravel or paving. Cut these plants back close to ground level in late autumn when they die back naturally.

♣ For a more formal edge that stays sharply defined, dwarf box is a favourite – it's slow growing and only needs clipping one or twice each year in April/ May and August/September.

♣ Alternatively, plant a fragrant row of lavender. Use compact uprightish kinds such as 'Hidcote' (some varieties are too big and bushy and sprawl too far over the path). Clip lavender edgings back tidily every year as soon as the flowers are over, in late summer or early autumn.

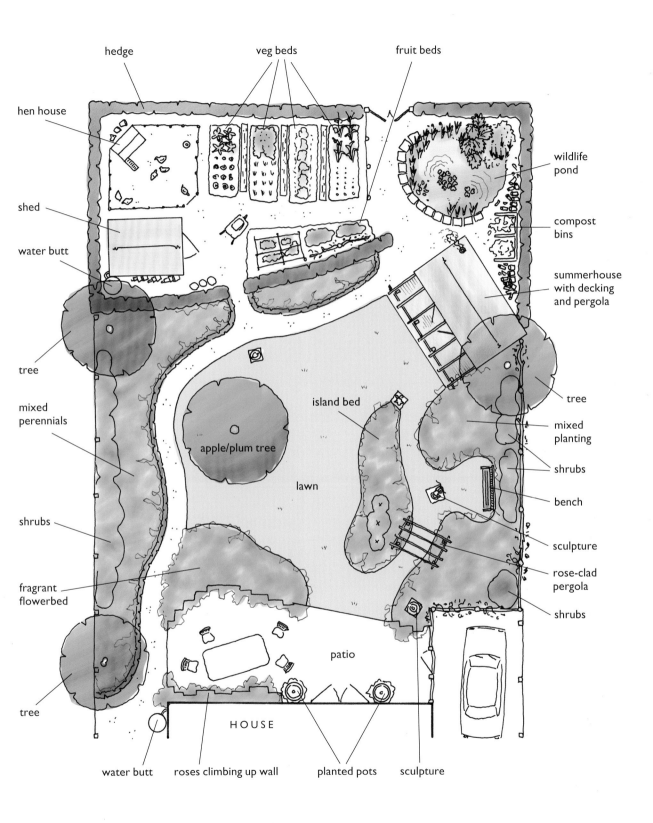

hedge

veg beds

fruit beds

hen house

wildlife pond

shed

compost bins

water butt

summerhouse with decking and pergola

tree

mixed perennials

island bed

tree

mixed planting

shrubs

apple/plum tree

lawn

bench

shrubs

sculpture

fragrant flowerbed

rose-clad pergola

shrubs

patio

tree

HOUSE

water butt

roses climbing up wall

planted pots

sculpture

Clockwise from top left: Roses need stout horizontal wires to help them scale a house wall; lady's mantle (*Alchemilla mollis*) is a country garden favourite; combine roses and honeysuckle for extra fragrance; plant tulips and forget-me-nots among summer-flowering perennials for a spring show; select a piece of statuary to act as a focal point; metal obelisks add height without being overpowering.

THE PLANTS

The essential must-have flowers for a country garden are **roses**, grown in mixed borders and up walls. Other key plants are traditional **herbaceous-border perennials** such as bearded iris, oriental poppies, phlox and lupins, plus old-fashioned hardy annuals, and herbs – especially dual-purposes ones such as purple fennel that look pretty as well as being useful in the kitchen. Today **colourful climbers** are also must-have ingredients, particularly clematis – plants you can never have enough of – and **fruit trees** and **veggies** are firmly back in fashion.

Create a self-seeding flower bed

A flowerbed that's made up entirely of self-seeding species is easy on the eye, good for butterflies and bees and needs little or no work. It also creates the perfect hotch-potch country look.

1. If starting from scratch, make sure the soil is totally weed-free, remove any roots and rubbish, then work in plenty of well-rotted garden compost.

2. Rake in a light dressing of general fertiliser such as blood, fish and bone meal to get the growing ready for sowing.

3. In late March or early April, sprinkle a mixture of old-fashioned annual flower seeds, such as love-in-a-mist, cornflower, poppies, godetia and foxglove, over the soil and shallowly rake them in.

4. As shoots come up, learn to tell weed seedlings from flower seedlings and pull out what you don't want before they get too big. Thin out the flower seedlings if too many come up.

Otherwise leave them where they are; self-sown seedlings develop far stronger root systems than flowers that have been dug up and moved, and they can withstand dryish summers better without needing so much watering.

5. Don't be too tidy; allow flowers to spill gently over the edge of the bed to soften the shape. For contrasting foliage, add lady's mantle (*Alchemilla mollis*) – a perennial that also self-seeds; the neatly pleated soft-green leaves and frothy lime-green flowers make a good backdrop to 'louder' flowers.

6. Plant box balls on the corners as a green all-year-round 'anchor' and to contrast with the floral chaos.

CLIMBING PLANTS

Climbers are vital ingredients of country gardens, grown around front doors, over porches, and on walls or over arches and pergolas. The top climbers for creating a country garden effect are roses (choose climbing or rambling roses), clematis and honeysuckle. They are incredibly versatile, and brilliant for making the best use of limited space in a small garden. Trained over trellis screens, they are a great way of dividing up one area of the garden from another, masking a vegetable patch or oil tanks and compost heaps, or for obscuring distant eyesores.

Climbers are also popular for growing up obelisks, rustic plant supports and pillars to give height to a border, and modern compact varieties of clematis (such as 'Crystal Fountain') make superb plants for growing all year round in large tubs, given a tall support framework to grow up. Many large climbers can be grown up through trees, which is fun as trees seemingly sprout a second set of flowers! It's also labour-saving as the climbers don't then need any pruning.

♣ Be wary of potentially huge, self-clinging climbers that may cause structural damage. Virginia creeper can damage mortar and weaken walls; wisteria is spectacular in full flower but grows enormous and needs a lot of regular hard pruning otherwise it goes mad and can damage guttering, downpipes and roofs by getting into gaps and expanding. As an alternative to real climbers for house walls, consider growing a wall-trained shrub or fan-trained fruit tree instead and tie the stems to trellis for support.

Plant a clematis against a wall

Walls create shelter and hold warmth, which makes them good places for climbers, but they do present problems that need special attention. Besides footings and builders' rubble, which soak up moisture, walls create a rain shadow area, so the ground at the foot of a wall is usually very poor and dry.

1. Before planting climbers, work in lots of well-rotted manure or garden compost to the whole bed, not just the immediate planting hole.

2. Provide supports. Screw vine eyes (which look like 15cm (6in) long metal skewers with a screw-thread at one end and a loop at the other) into the wall and use them to support horizontal wires over the area at one-foot intervals. Otherwise put up trellis.

3. Dig a planting hole and lower the rootball in. Plant clematis so the top of the rootball is 5–10cm (2–4in) below the surface of the soil. This allows plants to produce new shoots if they are affected by a fungus disease called clematis wilt, which kills the top down to ground level.

4. Water well after planting, using a whole large watering can. Clematis like their roots to be kept cool, moist and shady, so after planting place flat bits of slate or tile on each side of the plant to keep sun off the roots.

5. Don't try to untangle a clematis plant from the canes it was growing up in its pot, as the stems are very brittle. But when new shoots grow, tie them loosely up to the support wires or trellis with soft string. Clematis climbs using twining leaf stalks, so it's not long before new growth hangs on for itself – expect 1.2m (4ft) of new growth in the first year.

Rustic furniture

Outdoor furniture is a great way to underline your particular garden style. For a country look go for the sort of furniture that is intended to be left outside all year round since it forms part of the view, and choose suitably rustic materials and designs.

♣ Cast aluminium seats and tables are available that look just like original Victorian cast-iron garden furniture, ideal for a seating area. You'll need to add soft cushions, and they need moving under cover when not in use as they can get stained or go mouldy if they get damp.

♣ For family use, a picnic-type table and benches made from pieces of log can look very effective and are something any handyman can make. Position them in a patch of wildflower meadow or small nature area.

♣ Big benches make superb focal points down the garden; again antique-style cast aluminium versions are available, but you can also choose handsome natural hardwood benches or the decorative Lutyens-style with their distinctive-shaped fancy backs; these can be made from natural wood or painted white.

Create a cheat's mosaic

Stone mosaics give a garden an arts-and-crafts feel, and although they look elaborate there's an easy way to make them.

1. Half-fill a wide, shallow, plastic plant-pot saucer with fine sand and pour water in it till the sand is totally waterlogged and flattens itself out. Carefully tip the excess water away.

2. Use smooth, clean evenly-shaped pebbles and push them into the soggy sand in an attractive pattern – swirls or concentric circles are easiest but you can make animal or flower shapes.

3. When you're happy with the layout, set the saucer aside till the sand dries. Then pour quick-setting cement over the exposed ends of the pebbles, filling the plant saucer to the rim. Strike off any surplus cement level with a bit of board, so it's left smooth and flat.

4. When the cement is completely dry, tip the whole saucerful out like a cake and turn it over. The dry sand will have protected the tops of the pebbles so they stand out cleanly from the background cement.

5. Brush the sand off the pebbles and you are left with a round mosaic 'tile'. You can dot one or two around in gaps left deliberately in a brick or stone-paved path, or add several together to make quite large areas of mosaic.

Make an instant rustic boundary

If there's a gap in your garden boundary, or perhaps there's only a low wall, and you need more privacy, fencing is the quick solution. The usual interwoven fencing looks too 'townie' for a country garden, but there's a rustic alternative: hazel hurdles. These are modern versions of the home-made panels shepherds once used for temporary sheep pens, and are still made by the same method as the original old country craft, by weaving long, straight lengths of hazel between upright posts, a bit like basket making on a grand scale. (Something very similar is sometimes done using long, slender willow 'wands'.) Hazel hurdles are good at filtering the wind, and being slightly see-through they don't cut out all the light like a solid fence. They are also a lot easier to put up.

1. Stand the hurdle roughly in place to measure the spacing needed and hammer a strong post in at each end. The posts need to be sunk into the ground for about quarter of their length. (fig.1)

2. Angle another smaller post up against each of them as 'bracing', for extra strength. (fig. 2)

3. Cut several 30cm (12in) lengths of wire to use for securing the panels to the posts. Push one end of the wire through the edge of the hurdle and wrap it round the post; twist the ends together to hold it tight. Use a wire twist like this every 45cm (18in) from top to bottom of the post, and do the same for each post holding up each hurdle. (fig. 3)

4. A hazel hurdle lasts about eight years (occasional painting with timber preservative will extend its life), so plant a patch of evergreen shrubs or a row of hedging plants in front of it. By the time the plants fill the space the fence will have finished its job, but in the meantime it's helped the new plants get established and given you privacy and shelter too. (fig.4)

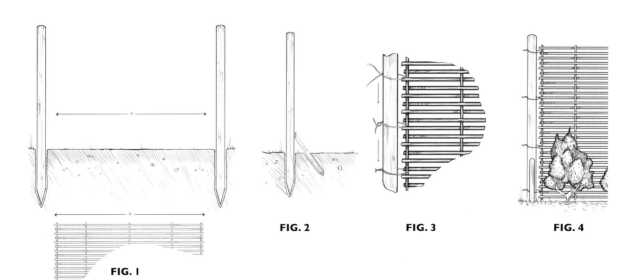

FIG. 1

FIG. 2

FIG. 3

FIG. 4

Make a rustic path

Stone or brick paths are a great feature of country gardens. You can 'get a man in' but if you are reasonably handy it's not difficult to lay your own.

1. Paths need sound foundations, but since they don't have to carry much weight these need to be a few inches deep. Excavate 10cm (4in) of topsoil from the site to allow for the 'footings' plus the depth of paving or bricks on top. The finished path should sit slightly proud of the surrounding soil.

2. For garden paths a couple of inches of rammed hardcore (broken bricks and concrete) can be topped with a couple more inches of mortar and the paving laid on this.

3. Sandstone and York stone are expensive, but nowadays paving manufacturers produce quite realistic-looking alternatives made from reconstituted stone. Cleaned-up second-hand bricks are available from architectural salvage yards and reclamation centres.

4. Instead of making the entire path or area of paving all of the same material, add detail to the scheme by insetting areas of pebbles set on edge into wet concrete to make patterns. Alternatively, try your hand at mosaic with broken pieces of pottery and china. The same techniques can be used on a large scale to make a seating area that matches garden paths and helps create a nicely unified look.

MAKE THE MOST OF A COUNTRY GARDEN – GROW UNUSUAL PRODUCE

Traditionally country homes generated a huge range of produce from their gardens, not just old favourites like potatoes and rhubarb, but also hedgerow fruit such as damsons, elderberries and sloes, long-forgotten herbs, and even edible wild plants that nowadays are little-known and hardly used. Today kitchen gardening is back in fashion and it's fun to rediscover forgotten culinary treasures, and grow unusual fruit and veg you can't find in the shops. You can also find novel ways of using them.

Lovage This is a herb whose leaves have a most unusual liquorice-curry taste – it's good for lamb or chicken dishes and great in chilled soups and salads. (It was once described as 'living Marmite' since the stems were chopped up and thrown into stews or casseroles, the way we'd use stock cubes today.) It is a strong, tall-growing perennial plant with yellow fennel-like flowers. It dies down each winter but grows back the following spring. It almost grows itself, is happy in partial sun or shade and looks good at the back of a flower border if you don't have a veg or herb patch.

Nasturtium These young leaves and whole flowers of this annual flower can be used as a peppery-tasting salad ingredient (best mixed with lots of blander lettuce; the flowers can be stuffed with cream cheese for variety). The tiny flower buds can be pickled and used as home-grown substitutes for capers.

Gooseberries This tasty fruits are easy to grow. Spread a good dose of manure round them in autumn and in winter prune the bushes so they keep an open cup shape; this encourages the plants to grow fewer but bigger gooseberries. Another tip for bigger better fruit is to thin out the berries slightly when they are Smartie-sized in early summer. Don't throw the 'thinned' fruits away as they can be used in cooking and have a sharp, tart taste. Leave the rest to reach full size. If you grow a dessert variety of gooseberry the full-sized fruit will be as big and sweet as a grape – you can eat them raw straight out of your hand, or use them in fruit salads.

Crab apples These are brilliant decorative trees for small gardens, but they can be made use of too. If you make your own cider, add a small proportion of crab apples to the mixture of cooking and eating apples used to make the juice that you then ferment. And for crab apple jelly – one of the very tastiest home-made preserves – grow the variety 'John Downie'.

Clockwise from top left: Lovage; Nasturtium, crab apples; gooseberries. These are all vital ingredients in the country garden when it comes to providing tasty alternatives to run-of-the mill food.

ENCOURAGE HEDGEHOGS INTO YOUR GARDEN

Loss of habitat in the countryside, and use of agricultural pesticides which kill off their natural prey, means today's hedgehogs are more at home in our gardens. They eat garden pests such as slugs and caterpillars, as well as beetles and worms, and they enjoy fallen fruit. Of course, there are several other ways to make your garden more hedgehog-friendly:

Create several hedgehog-sized access points; make little gaps for them to get through fences or under hedges, so they can move freely between gardens. The gaps need to be 12cm (5in) high and as wide.

Leave a few small 'nature areas' with wild plants or ivy in the base of hedges. Alternatively, just leave dead stems in your borders over the winter instead of tidying them up. These attract the invertebrates that hedgehogs feed on, and if there are plenty of dead leaves hedgehogs may also nest there.

Make a hedgehog feeder. Place an old rubber cat basket upside-down in a quiet part of the garden, put a brick on top to stop foxes turning it over, and half-block the entrance with another brick to stop cats getting in. Reduce the entrance to hedgehog size (12cm x 12cm/5in x 5in). Put kitten biscuits inside (which are small-sized cat biscuits), or buy special hedgehog food from pet shops and wildlife sections of some garden centres.

Put out drinking water. Use a wide, shallow, heavy bowl that won't tip over; clean it out and refill with fresh water regularly. Don't put out milk as hedgehogs are lactose intolerant so milk isn't good for them.

Avoid hedgehog hazards in the garden. Garden machinery, such as strimmers and mowers, cause injury or death as the creatures roll into a ball instead of running away when you are clearing long grass. Bonfires are another big risk – hedgehogs crawl underneath piles of rubbish and can't always escape in time if you set fire to their 'hideaway'. Always move rubbish to a new spot before burning. Slug pellets are also a hazard as hedgehogs may eat slugs that have eaten the pellets – use alternative slug remedies instead. If you find a sick or injured hedgehog, there are wildlife hospitals and hedgehog sanctuaries all over the country – find your nearest on the Internet.

SIMPLE STRAIGHT-FROM-THE-GARDEN SALAD

Preparation time
20 minutes

Ingredients
new potatoes
butter
spring onions, chopped
salt and pepper
balsamic or
    sherry vinegar
baby gooseberries
fresh lovage leaves,
    finely chopped

Method
1. Boil new potatoes in their skins, add butter, some fresh chopped spring onions, seasoning and a dash of vinegar (use a good balsamic or sherry vinegar).

2. For the finishing touch, toss a few tiny baby gooseberries and some finely chopped lovage leaves into the pan at the last minute.

3. Serve straight away; it's delicious on its own, but you can also enjoy it with chops or sausages.

CHAPTER 3

THE FORMAL GARDEN

*We usually associate formal gardens with grand stately homes –
the word 'formal' immediately makes us think of Hampton Court Palace,
or giant steam trains clipped out of yew, but those are both extreme
ends of a very wide and versatile style. 'Formal' is good for all sorts of far
smaller gardens, and you often see brilliant examples on a truly tiny
scale amongst the stylish 'designer' gardens at the RHS Chelsea Flower
Show. And though people think a formal garden must be complicated,
it's nowhere like as hard to create as it looks – in fact it's surprisingly
simple to do. You didn't even need to come top of the class in
geometry at school. The idea behind it is 'less is more'.*

Topiary is tremendously useful in a formal garden as it creates shape and form that exists all the year round.

WHAT MAKES A FORMAL GARDEN?

The essential ingredients of a formal garden are strong lines and axes as well as clipped evergreens, especially hedges and topiary shapes, plus gravel and paving. It's a style full of greens and straight lines with a few 'special' architectural features, such as classical or contemporary sculpture or water features, as focal points to catch your eye. The overall effect is seriously sophisticated. Be prepared for a lot of clipping!

Top tip: standalone features

Dramatic standalone features, such as metal obelisks, make great contrasts with plants. Stand them between clipped hedges or strong topiary shapes to create instantly theatrical effects. The stark shapes look like modern sculpture. Grow climbing plants up them for extra colour.

GET THE LOOK

THE DESIGN

If you've never thought you'd be good at designing a garden, formal is a good style to start with. It's all very pencil-and-ruler friendly, as you'll be playing around with shapes, angles and lines in very symmetrical ways.

Formal is a good style for a long, narrow plot as the space is easily divided up into a series of interconnected garden 'rooms' divided up by hedges, or screens of trimmed block-shaped evergreens that let light through the gaps. You can create either classical formal (yew hedges, box topiary, York stone and gravel with stone or terracotta urns and an antique-style fountain) or contemporary formal (trimmed bay or myrtle, potted lavender or rosemary topiary, shiny stainless-steel containers, glass water feature). You can also mix the two and still get away with it.

For a basic formal 'room', divide a rectangular area up into a pair of matching borders with a long straight pathway running down the centre. Plant the borders so they are roughly mirror images of each other. It's easy to do, and gives the area an elegant orderly look. Better still, divide a long, thin garden up into several 'rooms', creating narrow entrances between them so you pass from one area and one mood to another. A pair of trained topiary trees can be used as sentinels at either side of an opening and will focus the eye on distant focal points.

Repetition works well in formal designs; you could nearly-fill a small area with identical pyramid-trained evergreen shapes, or a series of different-sized blocks or spheres. Use only a few different species of plants to create each formal 'room' (less is more, remember). But give each 'room' a different planting scheme with an individual character, so each area within the garden looks different.

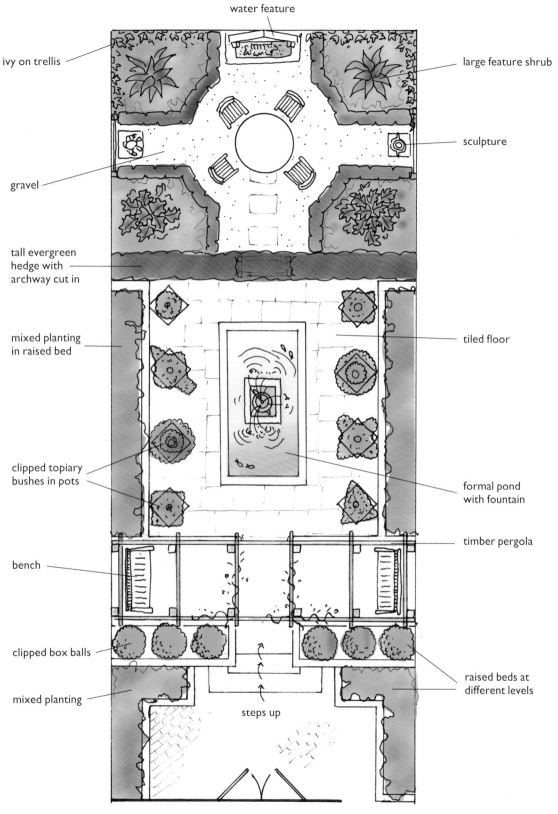

water feature

ivy on trellis

large feature shrub

sculpture

gravel

tall evergreen hedge with archway cut in

mixed planting in raised bed

tiled floor

clipped topiary bushes in pots

formal pond with fountain

timber pergola

bench

clipped box balls

raised beds at different levels

mixed planting

steps up

HOUSE

THE PLANTS

Symmetrical-shaped plants suit the formal style admirably – species that naturally grow into rosettes, bowls or spheres work well as they keep a good shape naturally without much, if any, clipping. Hostas (especially the large, strong-growing, blue-leaved kinds) are good for formal containers as they make a neat symmetrical shape. Being hardy, they can stay in the same container all year round, though they'll die down each winter.

Evergreen shrubs, particularly box and yew, are almost essential in formal gardens. Use them for hedging, or trim them into rectangular blocks or dome shapes grown in gravel or paving. Alternatively, train them into topiary shapes in the ground or in pots. A spiral, or a series of spheres on a bare stem – biggest at the bottom, smallest at the top – looks good. A matching pair will look dramatic standing one each side of an entranceway into a 'garden room'.

Ground cover can also be useful to set off bold evergreen shapes – choose low or short spreading plants to create a carpet that contrasts with larger neighbours. Lamb's ears (*Stachys*) is good for silvery-green colour and soft fluffy texture. It needs fairly well-drained soil and grows in sun or light shade. Variegated ivies can also be very effective and are good for creating splashes of gold or silver. Evergreen grasses or stripy-variegated sedges can be fun to plant thickly as textured carpets in contemporary formal gardens.

Green is the colour in formal gardens – it's visually neutral, which explains why a formal garden is so relaxing. Use lots of different shades of green, and as many shapes, sizes and textures as you can – shiny, felty, smooth, jagged, linear, bushy, frothy and ferny. Use other colours very sparingly – a tiny bit of white, cream, grey, silver, gold, or lilac here and there work together well for a cool sophisticated look. Colour can come from flowers, silver, gold or variegated foliage, background walls or fencing or architectural features such as statuary or benches.

Make good use of contrast, positioning coloured plants against dark wood, stone or brick walls, painted walls or green hedges. If you change the colour of a wall behind plants the effect can be completely different. To find colours that 'work' together hold a sheet of coloured card or paper up behind a set of plants.

Top tip: climbing roses

Wind the main stems of the rose round an obelisk in a spiral shape instead of letting it grow straight up to the top. This way it will have flowers all the way up instead of just at the tip of the stems. It's also easier to prune; just snip off the dead flowers plus an inch or two of the stem they grow from, all through the summer. Take out any dead stems in winter. Choose varieties that don't grow more than 3m (10ft) – 'pillar roses' are best for this job.

Create a cloud-pruned evergreen

A cloud-pruned evergreen makes a contemporary, modern alternative to traditional topiary. A ready-formed one costs a fortune from a nursery, but it's great fun to train your own at home and transform a fairly ordinary evergreen into a piece of living art. You'll see reasonable results straight away, and after three years you'll have a really good cloud-pruned plant. All sorts of evergreens can be used as long as they have bushy shapes, small leaves and lots of branching leafy shoots at the tips of the stems. Box works well, but also try conifers (cloud-pruning is a good way to 'doctor' one that's gone brown at the bottom), small-leaved privet (*Ligustrum delavayanum*) and myrtle.

1. Choose a good-sized, bushy plant with lots of foliage. (fig. 1) Start from the tips of the stems, leaving big 'blobs' of foliage there and working your way down towards the base of the plant using kitchen scissors or a small pair of secateurs. Cut away a lot of the lower sideshoots and foliage to reveal the bare stems. Don't trim all the way down to the bottom of the plant, and leave plenty of thick foliage so the bare stems branch out from a chunky-shaped leafy 'base' (a bit like flowers in a vase). (fig. 2)

2. Clip the foliage at the base of the plant into a dome or square shape. Thin out the bare stems, leaving a dozen or so nicely spaced out, choosing well-shaped ones that are nicely curvy. Trim the blobs of foliage at the ends into poodle-like pompons. (fig. 3)

3. Use hand-shears to clip the base three or four times a year so it stays neat. Trim box in May or June and again in late August if need be. Trim yew once a year in September or October so it stays looking crisp all year round. Trim the 'blobs' at the tips of the stems several times per season to keep them neat – use single-handed sheep shears for doing these small 'fussy' bits.

Top tip: DIY topiary

Start with a very dense, bushy box plant that's a good size but unclipped. Plant it in a large pot, sit a topiary frame over the top (various shapes available from garden centres) and trim the plant to the shape of the frame. Trim several times each season whenever the shape starts to grow shaggy. Dead easy!

FIG. 1

FIG. 2

FIG. 3

Grow hostas in tubs

Hostas are brilliant plants for growing in large pots or tubs – containers show off their shapes, and make it easier to protect the foliage from slugs and snails, which normally reduce them to ribbons when they're grown in the ground.

1. Plant in John Innes No.2 potting compost in spring; choose large plants – they cost more but make the most immediate impact. Keep the hostas well watered, and use liquid feed regularly from May to August.

2. Divide large plants in April when they outgrow their containers. Lift them out and prise the roots apart to make several smaller sections each with 3–4 strong shoots. Replant one in the original container with fresh potting compost and use the rest in the garden or to plant up other containers.

3. Use copper strips or plant protection glue round the side of the pot, or else stand the pot in a wide saucer of water which acts as a moat – being moisture lovers this won't keep the compost too wet, but it's enough to deter slugs and snails.

WATER FEATURES

Water features are a big asset in any garden. There are many types, from sophisticated, contemporary and minimalist, to natural-looking or the big showy, splashy sort. Choose the right kind for your style.

In a cottage or traditional garden good choices include a bubbling millstone or a giant piece of natural stone with water gently trickling out of the top. Choose the right plants to go around such a feature: ferns, hellebores, hostas and/or astilbes look 'right' with water and they put up with light shade and enjoy the splashes. They also allow the water feature to stand out and help to soften its surroundings so that it looks more natural.

For a city garden, choose a water feature with a more dramatic fountain effect, since the sound of running water is instantly soothing and helps blot out traffic noise. In contemporary gardens water features are often positioned to draw the eye. They can be quite complex, with perhaps a formal rill or an informal shallow gully filled with water winding its way through a paved area. Or you might opt for a 'reflecting pool' of shallow, still, standing water designed to reflect the sky and passing clouds, or surrounding foliage – with this it's vital to keep the water very clear, so don't put plants in the water, and use a dark material in the bottom of the water feature to maximise reflections. Black butyl pond-liner is fine, although garden designers at shows increase reflections by putting a little black food colouring into the water!

In a natural garden a wildlife pool looks good and it's great for attracting wild birds and mammals to drink. You can still keep fish, but go for hardy ones like goldfish (nothing fancy). Dig out a shallow saucer-like shape and line it with sand before laying a butyl pond liner. Don't position the pool right under trees as the leaves will foul the water.

♣ You might feel it's a big risk to have a pond if you have children, but it's not if you install a water grille. This is a strong metal grid that is fixed an inch or two under the water all over the surface of the pond. They're strong enough to stand or jump on, but not very noticeable when you're just looking at the pond, and waterside plants can still grow through them.

Create a water feature in a formal border

This makes a good focal point with a bit of sparkle for the end of a path, and you can easily add it to an existing area to gee it up a bit. The water feature shows up best with a clipped evergreen hedge or plain-painted close-boarded fence behind it.

1. Prepare the soil by clearing existing plants or weeds. Fork the area over and work in lots of well-rotted compost.

2. Place the water feature in the centre of the area so it's in line with the path leading up to it. It need not be anything complicated – a wooden half barrel or a ceramic bowl full of water is enough. A small fountain looks great but isn't essential.

3. Choose the right plants for the place. In a sunny spot with well-drained soil, lamb's ears (*Stachys*), cabbage palm (*cordyline*) and silver artemisia do well. In a moist, semi-shady spot hostas, ferns or hellebores are best. Use large plants for instant impact.

4. Stand the plants in position round the feature, turning each one round so it's best side faces the direction you'll normally see it from (every plant has a front and a back).

5. Plant everything properly, making sure you can still see the water through the foliage. The water adds

sparkle which lights up a shady area, and you should be able to see the reflections of the leaves in the water.

6. Trim existing evergreen shrubs surrounding the area. If there is a row of hedging behind the water feature, cut it a foot lower there to create a 'niche' immediately behind the water feature and its surrounding plants to make it stand out more from the background. The contrast of small-leaved evergreens, large-leaved hostas and water draws the eye, making this more of a focal point.

7. Outline the front of the water feature with low-spreading ground-cover plants to increase the effect – silvery-green lamb's ears create a change of shade and texture, and although they are usually thought of as sun-loving plants they'll be okay in light shade.

8. Mulch the exposed soil between plants with a thick (10cm/4in) layer of bark chippings to seal moisture in, deter weeds and set off the plants.

Install a water feature

For easy installation look for a small self-contained water feature kit where everything you need comes as part of the package. Kits usually consist of a reservoir to hold the water, a lid to go over the top, a pump, an outlet for the water to squirt or trickle out through (which often forms part of a decoration on the lid of the reservoir) and electrical wiring to run the pump.

1. Dig out the hole to take the water reservoir and make a narrow trench for the electric cable. Protect the cable by running it through a pipe – rigid plastic water pipe (as used by plumbers) is ideal. Place a few spadefuls of soft sand in the bottom of the hole and level it off.

2. Sit the reservoir in position in the hole and arrange the electric cable inside its pipe. Double-check the reservoir is level by resting a piece of timber across the top and sitting a spirit level on it – adjust the sand underneath until the reservoir is perfectly level, then back-fill the gap around it with more sand.

3. Connect the pipe running from the pump to the reservoir, fill it with water and put the lid on top.

4. When switched on, the pump pushes the water up through the nozzle in the lid so the water trickles or squirts out. The lid of the reservoir is bowl shaped and perforated so it collects the water and returns it to the reservoir, and so the same few gallons can be recycled endlessly. (It will, though, need topping up occasionally, especially if the weather is warm or windy – don't let the pump run dry or it may burn out.)

5. A small water feature looks good in a setting of gravel with a few plants such as ornamental grasses or sedges planted nearby. It can even look good when it's turned off if you choose one with a good-looking decoration on top, which is particularly useful in a small garden where every bit of space counts.

Make the most of a formal garden – plant window boxes

Get the formal look, even in the tiniest space, by creating matching evergreen window-box displays. Plastic window boxes cost less, and weigh less, than other kinds and they retain moisture best. Don't economise by using ordinary patio troughs – proper window boxes are very deep so they hold more compost, ideal for giving evergreen plants a long and happy life.

1. Put a layer of drainage material over the holes in the bottom of the window box – broken bits of polystyrene work well without adding to the weight.

2. Half-fill the window box with compost. Use a mixture of John Innes No. 3 and peat-free multipurpose compost, and for best results mix in some granular slow-release feed and some water-retaining crystals.

3. For each window box you'll need a small ball-trained box plant, four trailing ivies and a few white pansies. Plant the box ball in the centre (if it's a bit pot-bound tease a few of the roots loose so they can spread out once it's planted) and plant it at the same level it was growing in its pot.

4. Plant one ivy each side of the box ball, and another in each corner of the window box. Spread the trailing stems out sideways so they soften the straight edges of the containers.

5. Add the pansies. Don't plant them straight into the compost, instead plant two in a bottomless pot – squash the rootballs together slightly so they fit – and plant a row of these, pot-and-all, in the remaining spaces. When the plants are over, or if you just fancy growing something else, it's then very easy to lift them out and drop different plants into the same place without disturbing the other plants.

6. Water well. The secret of spectacular containers is to keep them well fed and watered. Because you've already added slow-release feed there's no need to use anything else, for a while, but do add another dose of slow-release feed next spring.

7. Lastly comes window-dressing. To complete the formal look, make up enough identically planted containers for all the front windows of the house, upstairs and down, so the same 'look' is repeated right across the front of the house. They'll make the house look incredibly elegant.

Top tip: formal containers

Space several large containers in a row each side of a central pathway through a formal 'room'. This looks showier than formal borders, and containers make far less work. Use the same plants in each container for maximum effect. Blue-leaved hostas look good in wooden half barrels and contrast well with an evergreen background. As an alternative you can use trimmed box cones in shiny aluminium cubes for a more contemporary slant on 'formal'. Another option is to grow a row of evergreen shrubs such as Mexican orange blossom (*Choisya ternata*) in terracotta pots – they'll still look formal and occasional light pruning will help them retain their natural domed shape.

CHAPTER 4

THE CITY GARDEN

You might think city folk rarely have the time or space to do anything really interesting in their gardens, but with a little creativity even the tiniest area can be transformed into a chic designer space that looks stunning all year round. A well thought-out garden makes a natural bolt-hole where you can escape from work pressures and city noise and bustle, and it's a great place to entertain friends.

Go with structured shapes, which complement the often long, thin shape of the plot. Boldness of form and rigidity of lines can be broken up by clever planting and by using well-placed plants in pots.

WHAT MAKES A CITY GARDEN?

Traffic noise and fumes, smells from fast-food outlets, late night revellers, litter, shade from neighbouring buildings and dreadful soil don't sound like the best conditions in which to create a dream garden. But don't be fooled, as a city has some huge natural advantages. The warmth from buildings creates a mild micro-climate (in London it's often 5°C warmer than out in the countryside) so a city gardener can grow slightly tender plants without needing extra protection. And when you grow bedding plants, veggies, herbs or salads, the same extra warmth means the growing season is several weeks longer in cities than in the countryside. City gardens lend themselves to an avant-garde approach – they are the natural environment for fashion-conscious trendsetters who are prepared to be adventurous in their quest for stylish surroundings. The challenge for city gardeners is how to make the best use of limited space without making the garden look cramped.

GET THE LOOK

THE DESIGN

Get rid of lawns as grass doesn't grow well in shade or on heavy clay soil (both common problems in city gardens). Instead have a central path with wide borders either side, and divide a typical long narrow city garden up into several separate 'rooms' – these can each have a different design theme. And instead of using a hedge or fence to divide a garden, go for things like a rill, a step, a low hollow-topped wall with alpines growing on top or a dwarf lavender hedge. It all helps make the space look and feel bigger.

Make a small garden seem more spacious by extending out into it from the back of the house. Do this by installing glass double doors opening out from the kitchen/diner or living room onto a paved area that uses the same paving as indoors – this makes the two areas flow seamlessly into each other.

If there's no room for a conventional shed, there are various timber 'garden stores' and sentry-box-style sheds big enough to hold the bare essentials. There are also very attractive sheds with gothic or rustic designs that are almost too posh to use for storing tools – so perhaps have a tool cupboard in the back of a tiny summerhouse for the best of both worlds. And gear your garden up with storage space in mind – if you don't have a lawn, you won't need space to store a mower, and if you buy weatherproof aluminium or hardwood garden seats and tables, and use a built-in brick barbecue, they can stay outside year-round.

A rainwater butt is handy for collecting rainwater off the roof and recycling it to water the garden (which is a big saving when you have metered water), but it can also double as a little raised water feature for keeping goldfish if the water stays clean.

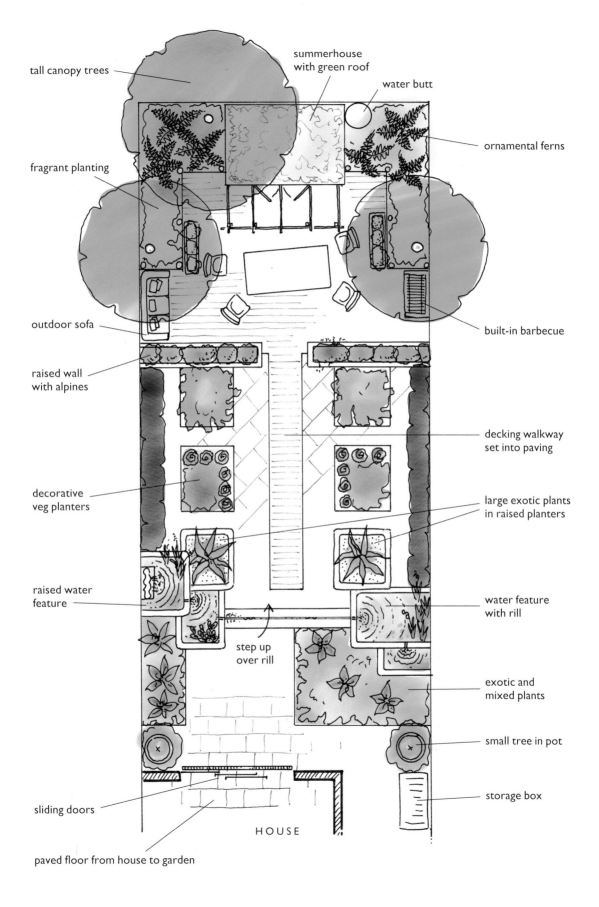

tall canopy trees

summerhouse
with green roof

water butt

ornamental ferns

fragrant planting

outdoor sofa

built-in barbecue

raised wall
with alpines

decking walkway
set into paving

decorative
veg planters

large exotic plants
in raised planters

raised water
feature

water feature
with rill

step up
over rill

exotic and
mixed plants

small tree in pot

storage box

sliding doors

paved floor from house to garden

HOUSE

THE PLANTS

To give a city garden a sense of privacy without it feeling too hemmed in, plant a canopy of **tall trees** to give part of the garden a leafy 'roof'– this creates lots of open space at ground level, but you can't be overlooked by neighbouring buildings. Avoid traditional trees, which will usually grow far too big for a small city garden. Instead use **large shrubs** that have been trained on single stems like trees; they add height to the garden, but they're easy to keep under control. Photinia is good grown this way. It's a naturally colourful evergreen with plum-red young leaves – especially in the variety 'Red Robin' – that contrast with the older green ones.

Alternatively, grow a small weeping tree such as *Cotoneaster salicifolius* – this only grows two metres high but has small leaves and lots of berries, so it attracts birds, looks good for more than one season and won't make too much shade. You could also **plant a screen** of pleached hornbeam – a single tree looks like a trunk with several straight branches growing out from the top parallel to the ground. People sometimes plant a row of these, which looks like a narrow hedge 'floating' 2m (6ft) or more above ground level on slender trunks, so you can walk underneath. It looks great and makes good use of space, but it's very expensive.

It's also possible to create privacy by growing **climbers** over a pergola or a structure of vertical and horizontal poles built-in to fill a space between buildings. This creates a **leafy roof** that gives privacy and shade to an outdoor seating or dining area. Climbers can also be grown over a decorative vertical section of trellis to create a quick screen – it grows faster than a hedge, and looks lighter and airier than a solid fence or wall.

Choose climbers that are a suitable size for the space available. Large, fast-growing species such as Virginia creeper or wisteria soon 'take over', need lots of pruning and shed lots of leaves. Something smaller such as clematis, passionflower, honeysuckle or a compact climbing rose are a better choice and also look pretty over a longer season (jasmine is the best climber for fragrance). Choose evergreen climbers such as evergreen *Clematis armandii* or *Trachelospermum jasminoides* (which has a jasmine-like scent) if you need a year-round effect.

When it comes to softening the overall scheme, plants are the answer. Even walls can be decorated with climbing plants that have attractive foliage and flowers.

SEATING AREAS AND FRAGRANT PLANTS

A secluded seating area makes a great place for entertaining, or just relaxing and enjoying the garden, and fragrant plants give it extra 'ambience'. A sheltered, west-facing area is the best place for a feature like this as it gets the evening sun, meaning it's also a great place to go after work. Choose a spot with a wall behind if possible, as this doubles as a 'radiator', trapping and reflecting heat; paving underfoot adds to the effect. It's the perfect place to set out sun-loungers or arrange your outdoor dining table and seats.

Use fragrant plants in the surrounding area. Pinks are great for raised beds and petunias are ideal for tubs or hanging baskets. Tobacco plants are also good because they give off their strong scent in the evening. Lavenders are quite powerful and can overwhelm more subtle scents, so don't over-do them.

Add some plants with aromatic foliage, too – they aren't reliant on flowers and their scented season continues far longer. They release their fragrance when you brush past the leaves, so plant them where they are easy to touch. Choose from fresh herby scents of sage or rosemary, or more feminine/fruity eau-de-cologne mint, lemon verbena and blackcurrant sage. Scented-leaved pelargoniums are also popular – these come in lots of deliciously scented varieties, ranging from pine, citrus and spices to rose. Any of these can be grown in tubs, troughs, raised beds, or well-drained borders in summer. Grow scented climbers such as roses, jasmine or trachelospermum over a warm sunny wall, or on an arbour above a bench.

CHOOSING GARDEN FURNITURE

Most of us buy garden furniture at some time in our lives, and since it contributes so much to our off-duty comfort and leisure facilities, it pays to take care choosing the kind that is just right for you. Before buying, consider how it will look in the garden, what is a suitable size, how much upkeep it needs and whether you can leave it outside all year round or if it needs under-cover storage. Outdoor dining sets need thoughtful selection. Make sure there is enough space all round the table to pull the chairs back fully with room to spare so people can get in and out (you don't want guests toppling off the patio into flower beds). To work out what's a suitable size, cut actual-sized templates from cardboard, like flat mats, to sit on the ground on the patio area, and take them with you when you go out to buy furniture. There is lots of choice from traditional to trendy contemporary.

Hardwood This is a very traditional material for garden furniture. It looks at home in an outdoor setting and can be left outside all year round. (Check for the FSC label to ensure that the timber is derived from sustainable forestry.) Natural wood weathers down to a pleasing colour and lasts well without being treated – oak goes silvery. If you want to keep the original look then use timber preservative with a natural wood colour, but do so in winter so the stuff has time to soak in, and won't mark your clothes. Follow the furniture makers' directions regarding suitable products.

Metal Whether traditional, antique or modern, metal furniture can be left out year-round. It may need painting after some years if the original white or coloured surface chips or is stained. Remove loose paint, dust and dirt, wash and when completely dry use an aerosol paint product designed for outdoor use on metal (these days they are eco-friendly).

Plastic This furniture is usually more economical, but can deteriorate if left outside for long periods in damp conditions, including over winter. It's also lightweight and blows about in windy weather.

Wicker and cane These are popular materials for furniture, but most suitable for the conservatory as they deteriorate in damp conditions. However some modern wicker furniture is actually made of a plastic material and can be left out without harm, though the cushions need to be kept inside when not in use.

Plant a tree

It's important to plant trees properly; they represent a big investment and if they die they'll leave a big hole in your planting scheme.

1. Water the new tree thoroughly before planting. If the compost was totally bone dry, stand it in a bucket of water for up to an hour, until bubbles stop coming out of the compost.

2. Lift the tree out of its pot and tease the roots out a bit, especially if the ball of roots form a very solid 'block'. Prise loose the coils of thick roots from the base of the pot with a hand fork and gently tease out small roots from the sides of the rootball.

3. Dig a planting hole that's slightly deeper and wider than the rootball of your tree, then check the depth of the rootball against the depth of the planting hole you've dug. Trees

and shrubs don't like being planted too deep – they should end up at the same depth they were growing in their pot.

4. Replace the soil around the rootball, firm it down gently with your foot and water very well. (Current thinking suggests that organic soil enrichment is unnecessary when planting trees since it results in sinking of the area around the plant, and the sooner the tree roots get accustomed to the existing soil the better.)

5. Give the tree a stake for support. Knock the stake in at an angle of 45 degrees and hold the trunk to it using a proper tree tie or an old pair of tights.

Create a green roof

Most gardens need a shed in which to keep tools, garden furniture and the like – the challenge in a tiny city garden is to turn what can easily be an eyesore into an attractive feature. A good solution is to paint the exterior woodwork a nice colour and add a 'green' roof. DIY green roofing kits cost around £25 per square metre from most good city garden centres.

1. Cover the roofing felt of your shed with a layer of eggbox-effect plastic. Next spread a layer of fluffy felty fabric on top of that and top it with an inch-thick layer of gritty compost. (fig. 1)

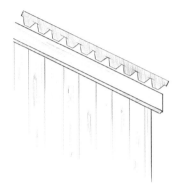

FIG. 1

2. Unroll special green roof 'turf' that's made of naturally drought-tolerant sedums. These come in various colours, including bright red, purple, autumnal brown or a mixture. The coloured kinds need a lot of sun and the green ones do best in shade. (fig. 2)

FIG. 2

3. A green roof like this covers plain roofing felt and helps the shed blend in with the garden. It's weather tolerant and reduces water run off – it also creates a mini habitat for birds and insects. (fig. 3)

FIG. 3

Make a decorative veg bed

A small fruit and veggie patch can make a worthwhile contribution to a city garden, and there's no need to hide it away if it's planted prettily.

1. Choose a sunny place, and if the soil isn't very good – especially if it's the usual horrid London-type clay – make a raised bed out of planks nailed to corner posts, or buy a ready-to-assemble kit.

2. Plant fruit and veg decoratively. There's no need to grow everything in long straight rows – organise it more like a flower bed. Make decorative obelisks for growing tall or climbing crops up such as tomatoes and runner beans.

3. Edge the bed with plants that are decorative and useful, such as red frilly lettuce, strawberry plants or short herbs such as parsley or thyme. Grow deep-rooted veg such as carrots in large bottomless pots or tubs filled with multipurpose compost standing on the soil. And grow colourful varieties of favourite veggies (golden courgettes, multicoloured rainbow chard, purple beans) – they taste as good (often better) than the plain green versions.

4. Also use large, free-standing veg planters on a sunny patch of path or paving. Some planters are very good-looking, and for real glamour look for matching 'living larder sets', which look like outdoor furniture. If you opt for growing bags, disguise them by piling pebbles around them or laying hessian sacking over the plastic.

5. Edible crops quickly suffer if they run short of water, so install a watering system, especially if you are busy, out at work all day or away at weekends. Attach a 'seep hose' to an outdoor tap and lay it out over veg beds so all the plants can be watered easily just by turning on the tap. It's possible to get timers that turn the water on and off automatically. For watering containers, use an irrigation system that has a series of dripping nozzles on short tubes coming from a central feeder tube. These direct water to each container individually without wasting it or making puddles all over your patio. Allow one dripper per pot and two or three drippers in larger containers.

MAKE THE MOST OF A CITY GARDEN – GROW BALCONY VEG

There are long waiting lists for city allotments, but all sorts of space can be used to grow edible produce, including window boxes, hanging baskets, balconies and indoor windowsills. One city gardener I met grows over 80 kilos of greengroceries on a balcony 3m (10ft) long and 1.5m (5ft) wide, which saves £500 a year from the family food bill.

All sorts of crops can be grown in containers. It's lovely to grow a few luxuries, such as **fresh green peas** or **baby new potatoes**. Broad beans don't give a big return from the space so just grow enough for one or two special meals, and make use of the bits most people just throw away such as pea shoots, pea tendrils and broad bean tops for salads. Crops that give the best return are high-value, fast-growing kinds. **Runner beans** are very productive, churning out more than 5 kilos from one container of plants growing up a wigwam of bean poles. **Mangetout peas** and **sugar, snow or snap peas** give far heavier crops than the sort of peas that you shell, since you use them pod-and-all. **Courgettes** are also very productive – choose bush varieties so they don't take up too much room, and cut them regularly while they are still small – this makes the plant produce more. **Chinese cabbage** produces the fastest growing 'greens', and you can be eating it after about 8–10 weeks. Surplus seedlings or young plants can be used as salad leaves.

It's easy to be self-sufficient in salads. **Baby cos lettuce** such as 'Little Gem' grows fast, and **cut-and-come-again lettuces** are picked a few leaves at a time so the same plants keep going for months. You can grow **watercress** in a trough standing in a tray of water so it keeps very wet all the time. Also good to grow are **rocket**, **baby spinach leaves**, **sorrel**, **red giant mustard leaves**, **endive** and **chicory** and various mixed salad leaves. In winter, go for special winter blends of mixed baby salad leaves. Also grow **fresh herbs** on the windowsills indoors – coriander leaves, chives, parsley, mint and chervil are brilliant.

Make a wormery

If you want to create compost in a tiny space a wormery is a compact, fast-acting alternative to a traditional heap. They recycle kitchen waste that would otherwise fill up your dustbin, turning it into rich organic compost. Buy a kit complete with the red brandling worms (don't use ordinary earthworms), and set it up in a sheltered corner, out of strong sunlight, and follow the makers' instructions. Add veg and fruit peelings (except citrus), leaves and trimmings, waste food such as bread and cooked veg (not meat or fish scraps), shredded paper and kitchen paper that's been used for wiping up spills (not chemical cleaning products). These are all digested by the worms and turned into rich worm casts.

Empty the wormery when it is full and use the fully rotted compost for filling containers to grow veg and flowers in. Restart the wormery using the material salvaged from the top of the container (which contains partly-digested material and most of the worms). If you don't like handling worms, use a three-tier wormery that consists of a stack of interlocking 'sieves' standing over a base on short legs – with this, you simply empty the bottom section and recycle it at the top of the stack without touching the contents. Use the liquid that drains out of the bottom of the wormery, diluted to at least half its strength with water, as a superb, natural and free organic liquid feed.

GARDEN SALAD

SERVES: 4

Preparation time
30 minutes

Ingredients
2 large handfuls of
   interesting mixed salad
   leaves, including some
   peppery ones like rocket
A few sorrel leaves
A whole handful of chives,
   chopped
Small scattering of
   just-pickled dill
A handful of mint
   leaves, whole
A small handful of lovage
   leaves, roughly chopped
4 eggs
200g bacon lardons
A splash of sunflower oil
1 slice of bread, cubed

**For the vinaigrette
dressing**
1½ teaspoons caster sugar
1 level dessertspoon
   Dijon mustard
1 small clove of garlic,
   very finely chopped
Salt and pepper to taste
2–3 teaspoons tarragon
   vinegar
3–4 tablespoons olive oil

The great thing about this salad is it uses whatever ingredients you've grown. You can use any combination of lettuce, sorrel, rocket, Chinese leaves, broad bean tops or pea shoots along with herbs such as mint, lovage, chervil, basil, parsley.

Method

1. Wash and dry the salad leaves (remove any dirt or bugs) and combine with the herbs in a bowl.

2. Boil the eggs for 6 minutes, then put them in cold water to cool before peeling.

3. In the meantime fry the bacon lardons with the splash of sunflower oil till they begin to brown.

4. Drain the lardons on kitchen paper, reserving the fat in the pan.

5. Fry the cubed bread in the bacon fat until crispy.

6. Chop the eggs.

7. Combine all the ingredients for the dressing except the olive oil.

8. Slowly beat the olive oil into the dressing until thickened and creamy.

9. Drop the eggs, bacon and croutons over the salad leaves.

10. Flick the vinaigrette dressing over the salad, toss and enjoy.

CHAPTER 5

THE FANTASY GARDEN

If you like a garden to be a magical place full of ideas and artistry, a fantasy garden could be just right for you. The space around your home is the perfect place to let your imagination run wild, and you can conjure up a scene from Narnia or Alice in Wonderland, or invent your own work of fiction. Like all good stories, a fantasy garden should be full of surprises – an adventurous journey through strange and exotic lands, meeting 'characters' en route, where the plot twists and turns to finish with a happy ending. It's pure magic, but it's not as difficult to create as you might think. And it's entirely do-able – even on a tight budget – when you're naturally creative and good with your hands

In a 'fantasy' garden there are simply no constraints on your imagination. Don't be put off by what others think – this is *your* space, to be used in a way that offers *you* pleasure.

WHAT MAKES A FANTASY GARDEN?

This style of garden relies on theatrical design and lots of details. It's created from extraordinary plants and elaborate decorations (found objects, outdoor art, knick-knacks and sculptures) all grouped cleverly to make a series of grottoes and little 'surprises' to discover as you walk around. A sense of secrecy is a vital element for creating a magical atmosphere – high walls are ideal so the garden feels detached from the real world. If you don't have them it's easy to create the illusion using fencing or hedges, or trellis screen planted thickly with climbers. You can be as over-the-top and outrageous as you like, although an artistic leaning and vivid imagination helps. As gardens go this sort is not in the least bit natural-looking, and for some tastes it's a tad over-planted and over-decorated – but it's the perfect play-space for a creative talent.

Top tip: fantasy scents

A fantasy garden should appeal to all the senses. You can use scented plants to create pockets of fragrance along your route, or cheat and add something purely artificial. Use a few drops of aromatherapy oils, perfume or other bottled scent, and sprinkle it onto a wad of moss, a saucer of moist bark chippings or just drip around the side of a plant pot – it won't last for more than a few hours, but it can be fun for creating atmosphere for a special occasion. Alternatively, use a scented candle burning in a lantern in the seating area (supervise so there's no risk of accidents). For a lasting effect hide the occasional air freshener dispenser out of sight, but avoid anything too 'polish scented' and choose a good-quality, lemony scented one.

GET THE LOOK

THE DESIGN

The key is that you don't see the garden all at once. Design the garden so that all the various features are revealed bit by bit as you walk around, to create an enchanted journey. That might sound like rather a tall order in a small garden, but it lends itself very well to the sort of long narrow plot that is found behind many houses in towns and cities.

The way most people deal with a long narrow garden is by running a path down the middle, or dividing it up into several squarish 'rooms' by cutting straight across the garden, but for a fantasy garden, be bold. Divide the space up using slanting lines to create irregular angular shapes. Going angular makes a small space look far more spacious.

Starting from the back of the house, create a 'journey' running all around the garden. You'll need a small area of paving immediately outside the patio doors, but it doesn't have to be rectangular – in keeping with the angular design elsewhere, make it triangular with the base running along the back of the house and the point up against one boundary. Create a screen across the back of your paved area so that you are enticed out to explore further. Use a row of brick pillars or strong timber posts that support swags of chain suspended across the garden to form a colonnade. Plant this with a strong-growing climber – wisteria is good as it drapes artistically and produces masses of long dangling heads of flowers along its length. From this, a dramatic entrance leads out to the start of the enchanted walk winding its way through a mixture of tall plants, strange plants and architectural goodies. This is where you can really let rip – every corner should be packed with incident and each gap in the foliage should reveal a glimpse of something strange and enticing.

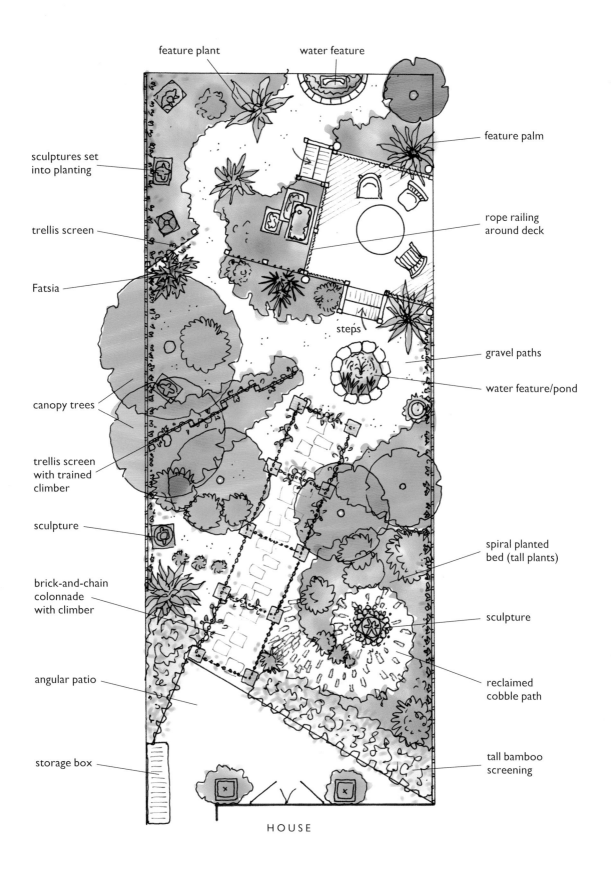

feature plant

water feature

feature palm

sculptures set
into planting

rope railing
around deck

trellis screen

Fatsia

steps

gravel paths

water feature/pond

canopy trees

trellis screen
with trained
climber

sculpture

spiral planted
bed (tall plants)

brick-and-chain
colonnade
with climber

sculpture

angular patio

reclaimed
cobble path

storage box

tall bamboo
screening

HOUSE

THE PLANTS

Invest in some spellbinding plants that look faintly other-worldly. Actinidia is a climber with pink and white splashes on the leaves. **A large tree fern** makes a real talking point with elegant arching fronds, but it's pricy – a grove of smaller ones also looks very effective. All sorts of striking **architecturally-shaped plants** are good – bamboo is a natural and some have thick, shiny or strangely coloured stems. Try fatsia, which has large, evergreen, fig-like leaves, and hardy ferns for lacy or frondy foliage which looks very fairytale. If you want trees with truly huge leaves for dramatic effects, go for the tree of heaven (*Ailanthus*), Indian bean tree (*Catalpa*) or paulownia, and cut them down close to the ground every 2–3 years; the result is a long, straight, upright trunk topped by gigantic foliage. Even the giant waterside plant gunner becomes curious, planted above a deep dip in the path allowing you to walk underneath and look up at the cathedral-roof effect of the leaves from below. Check out nurseries that specialise in architectural plants – they'll have a magical selection in stock.

Create **shady nooks** and niches in the foliage, and arrange ferns and rugged stonework round water to make **grottoes** – use them as backgrounds to set off statues, follies and artistic creations of your own invention. A frill of **ferns** or **ornamental grasses** makes a smallish collection of 'bits and pieces' really stand out; a background of **bamboo fencing** with ivies growing on it forms a good 'frame' for a striking ornament. Occasional sprites lurking in dense foliage or faces peering out from tree trunks adds a fairies-at-the-bottom-of-the-garden quality.

MAKING AN ENTRANCE

Build an arch Every theatre-goer knows the value of making a good entrance. A dramatic archway makes a wonderful starting point, and the moment you step through it you'll feel as though you are entering another world and embarking on a strange and wonderful journey in fantasy land. The arch must make an instant impression. All sorts of exotic bespoke designs are available, but can be costly, while more ordinary arches made of steel and plastic are sold for far less at garden centres. The cheaper arches still do the job nicely if you add a climber with bags of personality. Choose an unusual, interesting plant that won't grow too big, which has strangely shaped flowers and not too much foliage – a light delicate tracery of leaves is what's needed. The glory lily (*Gloriosa rothschildiana*) is brilliant – it's a temporary summer climber that grows from a tuber that has to be taken inside in winter (it starts from scratch again each year).

Buy two pot-grown plants, one for each side of your arch, and repot them into larger tubs so they have more room to grow. Half-fill the tubs with peat-free multipurpose compost, tip each climber out of its original pot and stand it in the centre of the tub, add more compost and use your fingers to firm gently down round the rootball. Leave enough room between the surface of the compost and the rim of the pot for watering. (Every time you water, fill the pot to the top so the compost gets a good soaking.) Untie the climbing stems carefully from the supports provided by the nursery – you'll be astonished how long these stems are when they're unwound. Spread them out over the arch and retie them gently in place. Within 24 hours all the leaves will have perked up and be facing towards the light so the plant looks as though it's been there for ever.

Create a curvy path This can lead from the arch around the garden. Make it double back on itself in several places so it disorientates you slightly and forces you to look left and right of your main direction of travel – you'll see lots of little nooks and crannies filled with detail this way. This is where all the odd angles created by the offset design of the

garden really pay off, as they automatically create lots of odd little shapes to be filled. The path needs to be quite heavily planted as it's important you can't see straight across it from one area to another. Use groups of plants, create banks of bamboos and use creepers to smother trunks of trees and boundary fences. Large climbers with showy leaves look spectacular in this situation – try the giant vine (*Vitis coignetiae*) which has huge dimply-textured leaves that turn bright reds and orange in autumn. One of the dangers of this kind of planting is that everything can easily look too dense and overpowering. Overcome this with the odd light and airy structure to act as a contrast with all the surrounding foliage. Also make full use of vertical space – obelisks, pillars and arches are brilliant on their own or planted with delicate climbers.

Journey's end Create something special at the top of the garden as your 'journey's end'. A small formal feature works well here, as a complete change from the very informal meandering character of the rest of the garden. You could create a clock garden with a sundial and a wall-mounted clock at the back of an area of paving and containers, or go for a crock-of-gold at the end of the rainbow effect. Fairy stories are a great source of inspiration (think toadstools, cobwebs and dewdrops) as is Harry Potter with his magic, dragons and broomsticks. Or why not try a 'lost world' with a bit of ruined temple, fallen idol and ramshackle hut? The world's your oyster. But be sure to include a seat, since you need a sitting place to soak up the magical atmosphere as your 'treat', and plan a different route back to the house so you aren't retracing your steps.

Make an instant grotto

If you have an existing bare section of dry stone wall or similar in your garden, you can improve on it immeasurably by giving it the grotto treatment – just add generous groups of plants along the base. It only takes moments if there's already a bed of half-decent soil. If the soil is poor, or there's just a solid path, plant up a large trough and stand that in place instead. Shade- and moisture lovers enjoy the conditions and have a naturally grotto-feel about them, so ferns are the natural choice. They are available in a wide range of shapes, sizes and textures – the Irish tatting fern is particularly striking, with 'knots' of tightly curled fronds dotted along the stems. Add bleeding heart (*Dicentra*) for a bit of spring colour – the flowers come in mauve, white or red depending on the variety you choose – and ivy is good for long leafy trails that soften the hard straight edges of the container.

1. Drill a few drainage holes in the base of a plastic window box or large plant trough. Spread several handfuls of gravel in the bottom to allow surplus water to escape.

2. Half-fill the container with multipurpose compost and arrange your plants in their pots to work out how they'll look best.

3. Give the plants a good watering, then tip them out of their pots and pack them into the trough – use lots, so the container is well filled.

4. Lift the trough into place. If you can still see the edges stand a row of old (even slightly rotting) logs along the front – they'll soon grow mossy and attractive.

Top tip: added sparkle

Dangle crystals at different heights from invisible mending thread or thin fishing line – they sparkle in sunlight and throw interesting spots and specks of light as they turn in a gentle breeze. Team dangling decorations with a group of small matching ornaments below them, at ground level – a series of terracotta orbs amongst low plants look good with a few suspended star and moon shapes just above them in the bushes.

Create a waterfall of flowers

A waterfall of flowers makes a fun feature that looks good in 'busy' surroundings with an existing background of foliage. It looks especially good where there are already moisture-loving plants (such as hostas), and a covering of pebbles, gravel and shells on the ground to suggest water. White marguerite daisies are a good choice of plant as they have lots of small frothy-looking flowers that suggest the foam of a waterfall, and they'll flower for most of the summer.

1. Choose several identical plants growing in pots, just coming into flower with lots of buds to come.

2. Sink some empty pots partly into the ground, and raise others up on bricks or wooden posts, arranging them to create a swirling shape that graduates up in height. (fig. 1)

3. Sit the plants inside the containers, and they'll create an instant cascade. (fig. 2)

4. Scatter pebbles and shells at the foot of the feature to replicate a beach at the base of a jungle waterfall, which sets the whole thing off. (fig. 3)

FIG. 1

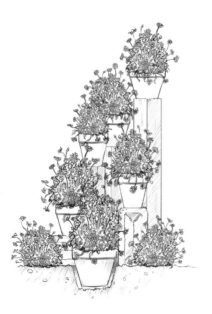

FIG. 2

FIG. 3

CHOOSING GARDEN SCULPTURE

Garden sculpture can exert a huge influence on the garden – a sundial, nymph, animal shape, large architectural urn or something contemporary can look great. The right piece of sculpture has a magical effect on the garden, but even a hugely expensive piece won't look special if it's in the wrong place, so think carefully before buying. Take a photo of the spot you have in mind when you go to buy, as sculpture needs to be in proportion to the place you put it. To work out the right size, stand different-sized cardboard boxes in the spot, or pile up several to make a bigger 'block', and see which looks roughly the right size for the space. Then measure the space they occupy so you know your size limits when you go shopping.

You can go for an original piece of outdoor art made by an artist costing thousands, commission a local ironmonger or get something from a garden centre. Alternatively, recycle something that may never have been intended as a garden ornament. Reclamation yards are good places to find unique items, and if they are chipped, rusty or stained that's all to the good as they'll look as if they have stood in your garden for ever. You can also save money by creating something unique of your own – some people do very well using twisted copper water pipe, or straight lengths of pipe hammered into the ground in groups, all at different heights.

Top tip: mix your styles

Feel free to use a wide range of different decorations in your garden. Astrological signs, lanterns, mythical beasts, contemporary metal objects, or natural-gnarled chunks of wood – anything goes. Each item or group of objects is seen in its own personalised setting, so you can't see them all at once. And don't be afraid to make changes; regard any bare areas or little 'cameo' features you've got bored with as an opening to try out a new idea.

A spectacular piece of sculpture is a good way to break up long straight lines in the garden or enhance a special view. It's brilliant as a 'full stop' at the end of a path, for sitting in the centre of a natural niche or as a focal point in a small enclosed 'garden room'. Normally a statue would be placed centrally in a niche or at the very end of a path to make a focal point. If you choose an animal statue you could stand it on grass at an angle off-centre, or even stand it half-hidden in plants so it looks as if it's just wandering out. If there's a place that gets a patch of sun at a particular time of day when you're home to enjoy it, stand the sculpture there so it's naturally lit-up.

MAKE THE MOST OF A FANTASY GARDEN – ENCOURAGE BIRDS

Birdsong adds a magical sound-track to a fantasy garden; the musical notes of songbirds lift your spirits as you walk around, while the sudden hair-raising squawks of woodpeckers and alarm calls of blackbirds give a sense of drama. The more birds you attract the more fantastic your garden will be.

You can be quite inventive about attracting birds to the garden, by being creative about the type of nest boxes and bird feeders you provide – they need not be the regulation kind. You'll find lots of ideas in second-hand shops, charity shops, stalls at village fetes and car boot fairs.

Novelty nest boxes Robins nest in all sorts of strange places, so hang an old kettle or leaky watering can inside a bush in a shady spot at about 1.2–1.5m (4–5ft) above ground level. Wedge or tie it firmly in place, with the spout pointing downwards so the interior can drain in case rain gets in. An old wire-framed hanging basket filled with moss will sometimes attract a wren to nest – hang it up high in a tree where it's surrounded by dense foliage.

Natural bird feeder Birds such as tits, woodpeckers and nuthatches often investigate rotten tree trunks as they are good places for finding grubs etc, so take a partly rotten branch you've pruned from a tree, or use a rotting fence post. Drill several holes all round, and up and down the entire length. Make some 'bird cake' by mixing lard or used cooking oil, raw porridge oats and birdseed with some bread crumbs, and press it into the holes. Hang the feeder up horizontally, like a swing, a foot or so below a fairly low horizontal branch on a tree. Birds will use it as a combined perch and breakfast bar.

Spa bird bath Water is vital for birds, not just for drinking – they also need to bathe regularly to keep their feathers in good condition, particularly in winter since feathers make natural downy insulation. Make a quick easy birdbath by sitting a galvanised dustbin lid upside down in a shallow depression in the soil. Surround the outside with small pebbles and place a few larger ones in the middle, so birds have a good landing site and somewhere to sit and preen. Clean it out often so the water doesn't turn green, and top it up daily. Dot a few tussocks of ornamental grasses all round – in pots or growing in the ground – to make it into more of a feature.

CHAPTER 6

THE FLOWER GARDEN

Flowers are what gardens are all about, for a good many people. The classic romantic flower garden appeals to all our senses and lifts our spirits — it's a blaze of colour, a symphony of scent and alive with butterflies and bees for six months or more every year. A well thought-out flower garden not only makes a stunning place to sit outside in summer, it generates surplus flowers to cut and bring indoors to put in a vase, and you can even harvest edible flowers to use for exciting culinary purposes. Creating a spectacular floral display may seem like a daunting prospect, but don't panic — just take it step by step.

Plant thickly and make good use of fragrant flowers so that the garden is as scented as it is colourful. A retreat among the blooms – like the painted summerhouse – allows you to enjoy the garden even in poor weather.

WHAT MAKES A FLOWER GARDEN?

A great flower garden is all about colour, and lots of it. When you step into a stunning flower garden, the effect is quite overwhelming – everywhere you look there are wall-to-wall flowers. But once you look harder, you'll see there's a little order. Lavish banks of blooms are divided up by meandering paths, and punctuated by occasional architectural features such as obelisks or a home-made pergola made from rustic poles (which themselves double as excuses for growing taller flowers that need support). A lawn and hedges are the only 'extras' needed to show off colourful displays of flowers perfectly, though you'll need a well-placed seating area from which to enjoy the panorama of fragrant, glamorous views. When it's well planned the show continues without a break from early spring to late autumn.

Top tip: border design

Use a combination of curvy borders round the edges of the garden, and informal (perhaps teardrop shaped) island beds cut out of grass or surrounded by gravel paths inside the area.

GET THE LOOK

THE DESIGN

Think of a jigsaw puzzle; a series of interlocking 'bits' with curvy sinuous shapes that all fit together to make one big picture – that's what you are aiming for with a flower garden. The difference is it's a 3D puzzle, so after planning out the shapes of your beds and borders on paper, with winding paths inbetween and perhaps a lawn for contrast, create a planting plan so you know which plants will go in the spaces.

Besides the usual considerations of choosing plants that like sun or shade, and damp or dry soil, think also about height. The key to creating a great flower garden is to arrange plants so they graduate in height like pot-plants on tiered staging in a greenhouse (or if you prefer, think of cupcakes on a tiered cake stand), so that each one can be properly seen. And make sure adjacent colours don't clash – the best ways to do that are to use plenty of leafy foliage plants between flowers, and to limit yourself to a few complementary colours instead of going for a full-on mish-mash with everything thrown in.

As a final complication, you also need to plan for changing seasons. You won't find one set of flowers that will stay in bloom constantly from spring to autumn – it will take at least three different kinds to fill the season, even if you choose long-flowering types. It's not easy to keep one border – even a large one – packed with colour continuously over three seasons, so what most flower gardeners do is create one large border with an assortment of spring, summer and autumn flowers dotted evenly throughout it, and then make smaller beds that 'peak' at particular times, such as spring or autumn.

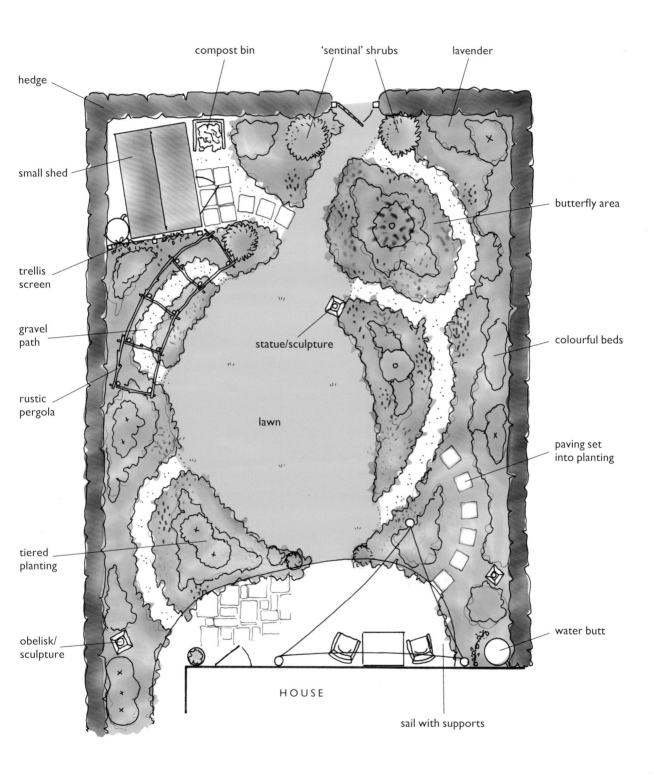

compost bin

'sentinal' shrubs

lavender

hedge

small shed

butterfly area

trellis screen

gravel path

statue/sculpture

colourful beds

rustic pergola

lawn

paving set into planting

tiered planting

obelisk/ sculpture

water butt

HOUSE

sail with supports

THE PLANTS

Flowers fall loosely into two camps: annuals and perennials. You need a mixture of each to create a fully flowery effect that stretches over the whole summer. **Perennials** live for many years and get bigger every season, and include old favourites such as delphinium, peony, lupins, penstemon, phlox and scabious. They are mostly bought as established, **pot-grown plants** from a nursery or garden centre and can be planted even when they are in flower, for instant results.

Annuals grow, flower and die all in the same year, and they'll usually bloom constantly for 3–6 months – they make a stunning show in their short lives. **Hardy annuals** are the simplest and cheapest to grow, and include clary sage (purple), pot marigold (orange), larkspur (deep blue), cornflower (bright blue), poppies (mixed bright colours) and nasturtiums (orange). They come up and bloom, then they produce seedheads which naturally sprinkle their contents around so they re-sow themselves for another year.

Top tip: add height

Get a tiered look by growing tall flowers on structures such as pergola poles, arches and obelisks, and under-plant the fronts of beds and borders with spring bulbs and shorter ground-cover plants.

Plant perennials

Perennials are, without doubt, the stalwarts of the flower garden. They can be in bloom from early spring to late autumn and they provide bulk as well as colour. A few shrubs among them will provide stature – all year round if they are evergreen – but the perennials will be the front-line performers for most of the year and offer brilliant value for money.

1. Work plenty of well-rotted compost into the ground and remove any weeds. Water the plant well.

2. Dig a hole in the prepared ground that's slightly bigger all round than the plant's pot. Tip the plant out by turning the pot upside down, placing the fingers of your other hand each side of the plant to stop if falling out and tapping the bottom of the pot to loosen the roots – you can easily then lift the pot off the rootball.

3. Turn the plant up the right way and stand the root ball carefully into the planting hole – there's no need to tease the roots out at all. The surface of the compost in the pot should sit level with the surface of the soil in the border.

4. Tumble loose soil into the gaps round the edge of the rootball to fill in the hole, then use your fingers to firm down gently. Finish off by giving the plant another good watering to settle it in.

Top tip: useful foliage

Use plants with interesting textured, variegated or coloured foliage (such as heucheras) to give groups of flowers a good background or foreground, and to separate potentially clashing colours.

Sow hardy annuals

Growing your own hardy annual flowers from seed is very easy. Some kinds can be sown in autumn, to give early flowers, but they are usually sown in spring, around March or early April (or later if the weather is cold). The earliest sowings will start flowering in May or June.

You can sow hardy annuals where you want them to flower; this is best for plants such as poppies that don't like being transplanted – just thin the seedlings out if too many come up. Other kinds of hardy annuals can be sown in a spare bit of ground and then dug up and replanted where you want them to flower.

1. Choose a sunny patch of ground and clear away any weeds. Fork it over and rake it to a crumb-like texture. Turn the rake over and push the back of it lightly into the soil to make a series of shallow grooves about 1cm (½ in) deep and 10–15cm (4–6in) apart.

2. Empty the seeds out of the packet and into your hand. Take tiny pinches of seed between finger and thumb and sprinkle them thinly along the grooves, rather like putting salt on your fish and chips.

3. Turn the rake back the right way up and lightly pull the earth back into the grooves – don't over-do it as seeds won't come up if you bury them too deeply.

4. Water the seeds in using a watering can with a fine rose fitted to the spout. This avoids washing the seeds away (a hose is too powerful). If the weather is wet leave the rain to do the watering for you.

Top tip: plant supports

Use stakes to hold tall weak delphiniums upright and prevent them breaking in bad weather. Use plant support frames to hold floppy medium-sized plants, such as oriental poppies, tidily in place.

Top tip: fill every space

Don't leave any bare soil showing. Plant groups of annuals to fill gaps between permanent plants, and if a gap appears during the summer stand a pot of flowers in place – lilies, alstroemeria or dwarf dahlias are all great for this job. Keep a few handy on the patio for emergencies.

ATTRACTING BUTTERFLIES

A spectacular flower garden is a magnet for butterflies, but some plants in particular are well known for attracting them. As a general rule, butterflies like visiting single, simple flowers, preferably native species or ones close to them – blooms that have been especially bred for big blowsy double flowers have often lost their nectar and pollen-making parts so there's nothing to interest butterflies or bees. Some of the best butterfly plants include the butterfly bush (*Buddleja davidii*), ice plant (*Sedum spectabile*), scabious, marjoram and Michaelmas daisies. They'll also visit other flowers such as astrantia, cosmos and daisies along with old-fashioned hardy annuals.

Flowers provide nectar for fully grown butterflies, but other plants provide food for their caterpillars, so if you want your garden to host the entire family it's only fair to provide food plants too. A clump of nettles is the perfect crèche as it can house up to five different kinds of caterpillars over a single season. People worry about caterpillars eating their favourite plants, but in practice the kind of caterpillars that feed on ornamental garden plants are only found in tiny numbers and they spread themselves out over the whole plant so they don't do too much damage. The only caterpillars you are likely to find in damagingly huge numbers tend to be species that are pests of cabbages, or of gooseberry bushes (though the mullein moth can wreak havoc on verbascums and Solomon's seal can be totally denuded by sawfly larvae).

♣ Regard it as doing your bit for conservation! Find out more about butterflies at www.butterfly-conservation.org

Create a sail canopy

The most popular place to sit and enjoy the views over a stunning flower garden is from a seating area outside your back door. It's usually one of the sunniest places, and being sheltered by the walls of the house it forms a natural suntrap. But on scorching days in midsummer it can sometimes be a bit too much of a good thing, and a little shade can be very welcome. Some people might build a pergola along the back of the house with wooden 'rafters' to grow climbers on and create shade over their seating-out space, which looks very 'folksy'. Others might opt for the temporary solution of a parasol. But for a very stylish contemporary alternative you might consider putting up a shade sail. This looks like a small sail from a sailing boat, specially produced to use in the garden for shade (find suppliers online).

1. Drill a couple of holes in the house wall above the patio doors, 2 metres high and 4 metres apart, and fix an anchor hook in each hole. (fig. 1)

2. Dig a hole 60cm (24in) deep on the other side of the paved area, at about the midway point. This will take a 3.5m (11ft) anchor post. (fig. 2)

3. Stand the post in the hole and wedge bits of old broken paving slab down the sides to keep it steady. Use a spirit level to check it is properly upright, then fill the hole with post-mix concrete – shovel this into place while it's dry, and then water it with a can once it's in place. (fig. 3)

4. When the concrete has set fill the rest of the hole with soil. Attach another hook to the anchor post, like the ones in the wall.

5. Plant a showy annual climber, such as morning glory or purple bell vine (*Rhodochiton*), in a tub and place it at the bottom of the post. Tie the stems in place to mask the post. (fig. 4)

6. Plant the surrounding space with fragrant flowers such as lilies and lavender to perfume the whole seating area. (fig. 5)

7. Surround all the new plants with pea shingle which acts as a Mediterranean-style mulch, sealing moisture in the soil and deterring weeds. It also 'ties' the planting in visually with the existing paving slabs, making more of a continuous look.

8. Attach the shade-sail to its anchor hooks to create a stylish canopy – it couldn't be simpler! (fig. 6)

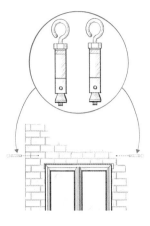

FIG. 1

FIG. 2

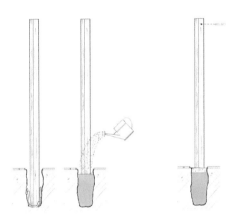

FIG. 3

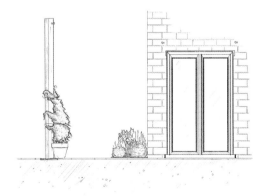

FIG. 4

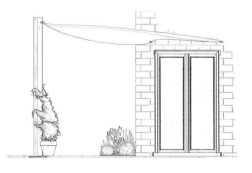

FIG. 5

FIG. 6

Make a gravel path

The thing that holds a packed flower garden together is its network of paths, which weave between the beds and borders. Gravel makes a hard-wearing, all-weather surface and gives a nice natural look that also sets off the flowers well and stops them being splashed with mud in rainy weather. What's more, gravel paths are cheap and quick and easy to lay yourself. Use washed pea shingle in the traditional buff-colour, available by the cubic metre from builders' merchants. (You could use white gravel, crushed granite or other forms of decorative gravel, but expect to pay more.) You can lay gravel straight over bare soil; use a layer 5–8cm (2-3in) deep. It's enough to deter most weeds, but any flowers in the area will shed seed into the gravel and some will grow. This isn't usually a problem as you get lovely naturalised colonies of flowers softening the shape of your path.

1. Mark out where you want to lay the path. Clear any weeds or strip off the existing turf, then level the ground and firm it down well with your feet.

2. If you struggle with perennial weeds cover the soil with a layer of weed-proof membrane before spreading the gravel – the fabric lets water through, but won't let weeds come up. Spread the sheet over the area and stretch it taut, then spread a three-inch layer of gravel out over the top. The membrane won't show unless it gets scuffed up.

3. For a neater, well-defined path, use a row of bricks to edge the sides of the path, otherwise let the gravel 'flow' gently into surrounding flowerbeds.

4. Remove any weeds or unwanted self-seeded flowers by hand, or rake over the surface of the gravel occasionally to prevent seedlings growing – this also smooths out footprints or tracks left by bikes and barrows. Don't rake gravel paths with weed-proof membrane underneath as you risk snagging the plastic and pulling folds up to the surface.

5. Gravel paths usually need topping up slightly every few years, as gravel 'walks' into flowerbeds or sinks into the ground due to the action of earthworms. But a thin surface scattering is usually enough to top-up and freshen the look.

Top tip: pyramid bed

Plant a large island bed with tall grasses or evergreens in the middle, medium-sized flowers in front of these, and grow short plants and carpeting kinds round the base. This looks good seen from any angle as you walk around it.

MAKE THE MOST OF
A FLOWER GARDEN – GROW
FLOWERS FOR CUTTING

All sorts of flowers are good for cutting – sweet peas are old favourites but a mixture of annual country flowers such as larkspur, cornflower and calendula marigolds jumbled in a plain enamel or china jug looks stunning on the breakfast table or on a windowsill. Many perennials such as delphiniums, alstroemeria and pinks also make good cut flowers, as do roses.

Keen arrangers will often grow a special bed of flowers for cutting, or they'll plant a few rows of annuals in the veggie patch, to avoid spoiling displays in garden beds and borders. But it's easy to cut small quantities of flowers from beds without spoiling things – simply snip flowers from places they won't show (the back of a plant, or the centre of a bed) and don't take a whole bunch from one place as it will leave a very obvious gap. When you're cutting, only cut perfect flowers, and don't take more than you really need for your vase to avoid wastage. Make good use of foliage (heuchera, pittosporum, eucalyptus, hostas, ferns) so that a few flowers go a long way.

When you get indoors, stand the flowers in water straight away to keep them fresh till you have time to arrange them. Dissolve a teaspoonful of sugar or use a sachet of cut flower food (from florists' shops) in the vase to make blooms last longer.

Top tip: edible flowers

Some flowers don't just look good – they also make fantastic culinary ingredients. Edible flowers include chives, lavender, sunflowers, pinks, violas, nasturtiums and thyme. Pull the individual petals or tiny florets carefully away from the green bases of the blooms (the green bits taste bitter) and scatter on green salads. Some flowers can be crystallised (whole violet flowers, or individual rose petals are best). Dip them in egg white then sugar, and leave them to dry thoroughly. Use them to decorate cakes and trifles. You can also find recipes for treats such as rose-petal jelly in old-fashioned cookery books.

LAVENDER CHOCOLATES
MAKES 50 CHOCOLATES

Preparation time
3 hours
Suitable for freezing

Ingredients
30g blossom honey
75g double cream
1 vanilla pod
3–4 fresh lavender flower
heads, or 5–6 dried heads
100g butter
130g dark chocolate

To finish
200g dark chocolate,
for dipping
75g cocoa powder

Method

1. Place the honey and cream into a small saucepan on a low heat, beat together gently, stirring till they come to the boil.

2. Split the vanilla pod and place it in a bowl with the lavender flowers.

3. Pour the warm honey and cream mixture over them. Set aside and leave to cool for at least two hours, or cover the bowl and leave in the fridge overnight.

4. Lay a piece of muslin in a bowl and pour the honey/cream/vanilla pod/lavender infusion over it. Strain the mixture through the muslin and discard the flowers and pod (the muslin can be washed and reused).

5. Fill a saucepan one-third full of water and heat to simmering point. Place the dark chocolate in a heatproof bowl and stand this over the saucepan of simmering water. Stir constantly while the chocolate gently melts.

6. Use a cloth to remove the bowl from the saucepan and continue stirring the chocolate while it cools slightly.

7. Pour the melted chocolate into a bowl with the cream/honey/flower infusion, and beat them all together till thoroughly combined.

8. Add the butter to the mixture and beat until it stiffens slightly and holds its shape (soft peaks).

9. Now either refrigerate the mixture and when it's completely cool form it into dollops with a teaspoon, or else use a piping bag to pipe blobs onto a tray lined with greaseproof paper.

10. Cover and place in the fridge – they can be left for up to a couple of days until you are ready to coat them.

Dipping

1. Melt the chocolate using the same method as above (i.e. heatproof bowl over simmering saucepan of water).

2. Use a cloth to remove the bowl from the heat and stir the chocolate till it's just tepid but remains melted.

3. Take the lavender chocolates from the fridge – use a fork to dip each one into the melted chocolate, ensuring each one is completely coated.

4. Place the cocoa powder in another bowl and drop each chocolate into the powder, again making sure each one is completely covered.

5. When the coating is firm enough to handle, shake off excess cocoa powder and place the chocolates on a tray lined with greaseproof paper.

6. Return the chocolates to the fridge to set fully. They'll keep for up to one week. They taste like standing next to a lavender hedge on a warm day!

CHAPTER 7

THE ENTERTAINMENT GARDEN

When you have a young family, lots of friends and a house that's bursting at the seams, the garden makes valuable overflow space. But don't leave things to chance – design it as an outdoor living-cum-dining room that makes a natural 'green' extension to your home. This is the perfect solution for anyone who wants a multi-functional garden. With thoughtful design, well-considered planting and a few hidden extras, it can easily become everyone's favourite party destination. But even when you're home alone, a garden like this is a brilliant place to sit and unwind – soothing water and calming colours are a great aid to relaxation. It's the ultimate stress-buster.

Clockwise from top left:
All-weather wicker furniture is fantastic for entertaining in style; candles provide romantic, low-key lighting on a summer evening; a varnished timber gangway leads from house to entertaining area; purple walls add a dramatic contemporary feel and show off green foliage exceptionally well; a table and umbrella makes the simplest entertainment area.

WHAT MAKES AN ENTERTAINMENT GARDEN?

Good looks, comfort and quick, easy upkeep are the hallmark of this sort of garden. Expect to see luxurious garden furniture, elegant outdoor dining sets, top -of-the-range barbecues and wonderful planting that makes a theatrical backdrop. Child-friendly features, outdoor lighting and fascinating 'conversation pieces' all help give a garden like this a warm, friendly feeling that encourages socialising.

Top tip: the perfect party

If you're holding a big party – perhaps to celebrate a family event – it pays to take steps above and beyond what you'd do for more casual entertaining. Hire high-class portable loos – it saves lots of people tramping constantly through the house and avoids queues. You'll need to park them on the drive or grass with hard-standing (a level site is essential). Also hire extra glasses, or buy sets of cheap ones from a discount hardware shop, and put up a mini marquee in case of bad weather. Consider calling in an outside catering company, or use a local cook who caters for events or big dinner parties on the spot. And don't forget parking if there's not much space outside the house – make an 'arrangement' with a local village hall or church in exchange for a donation.

GET THE LOOK

THE DESIGN

The first essentials are privacy and shelter – no one enjoys being overlooked by the neighbours or buffeted by a chilly breeze when they are sitting and relaxing. Turn the space into a secluded sun-trap by making full use of walls and fences, and if need-be add trellis structures with climbers growing on them.

Grass gets a lot of heavy wear in a 'party' garden, so paving makes a far better all-weather surface and needs less upkeep. Choose furniture that's designed to be left outside, so that you're always ready if friends drop round unexpectedly – just bring out some cushions and pour the drinks!

Design the garden as a number of small, separate seating areas that lead naturally on from the house – this is a good design ploy for making the best use of a long narrow garden. Organise a focal point at the far end of the garden, so that people need to walk down to investigate; a dramatic sculpture or eye-catching tree does the job nicely, especially if it's lit up at night. A fragrant herb garden containing unusual varieties, a striking sculpture or strange tree will all help to get people chatting.

If there's a natural dip in the ground, turn it to your advantage by making a semi-sunken garden. It's clearly not going to work in a wet corner – you need very well-drained soil – but given gravely soil it only takes a few seats round the edge, and a special feature in the centre (perhaps a water feature or a brazier), to turn it into a conversation pit.

Opt for a few striking raised beds – they'll need far less upkeep than conventional borders, and raised beds can also double as built-in seating – just keep a supply of cushions handy. Introduce colours on rendered boundary walls – a few hours redecorating is all it takes to create an inexpensive new look when you feel like a change.

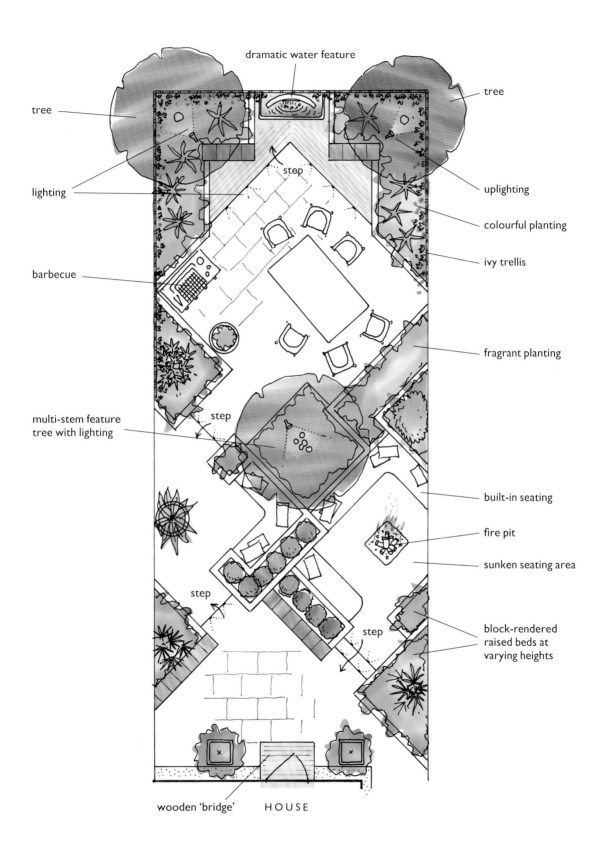

dramatic water feature

tree

tree

uplighting

lighting

colourful planting

ivy trellis

barbecue

step

fragrant planting

multi-stem feature
tree with lighting

step

built-in seating

fire pit

sunken seating area

step

step

block-rendered
raised beds at
varying heights

wooden 'bridge'   HOUSE

Bridge the gap between house and garden

Make a seamless transition between your kitchen or living room and your garden. Instead of the usual step down onto the patio (which is rather high risk if Auntie has had one sherry over the odds) make a 'bridge'. This acts like a gangplank to a millionaire's yacht and gives guests a dramatic introduction to your glamorous garden. A stylish tropical hardwood walkway made of iroko may be out of your price range (always check that it is from sustainable sources), but it's not difficult to make your own cut-price version using materials from any builders' merchant. When all the timber is cut, expect it to take about half an hour to build.

1. For a simple bridge take two lengths of what handymen call four-by-two. Stand them on edge, parallel to each other and about 40cm (16in) apart (or however wide you want your walkway) – these will be the 'rafters' that hold the whole thing together. (fig. 1)

2. Arrange pieces of decking timber cut to length across the rafters – allow a 3cm (1¼in) overhang each side, so you can't see them when the walkway is finished (it's a handyman's tip that gives a more professional-looking finish). (fig. 2)

3. Allow small gaps in between the decking planks (it looks better and means rainwater can run away quickly, so the walkway won't be slippery). Use a piece of thin timber as a spacer, so there's an equal-sized gap of perhaps 1cm (½in) between planks.

4. Double check the decking planks overlap equally on both sides of the rafters. Drill two sets of screw holes each end going through the decking pieces and into the rafters. Fit a countersink end on the drill so the screws can be sunk down into the wood so you don't catch your feet on the tops.

5. Use 9cm self-tapping wood screws to fix the decking to the rafters. Proceed from one end of the walkway to the other, using the same spacer so each cross-plank is exactly the same distance apart and checking that the rafters are parallel. (fig. 3)

6. Stand the 'bridge' on a firm path or half sink bricks into gravel as a solid base. Paint the woodwork all over with water-based timber preservative – re-treated every year, it should last a decade.

FIG. 1

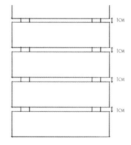

1CM
1CM
1CM
1CM

FIG. 2

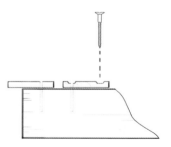

FIG. 3

Hardy geraniums and carpeting plants such as the toughest herbs make good edging plants and front-of-the-border fillers in any garden.

THE PLANTS

However well designed and luxuriously appointed it might be, a sociable garden would seem cold and lifeless without plants – the **shapes and textures** of foliage help soften the hard lines of paving, raised beds and furniture, and flowers look cheery and 'lift' the whole thing to another level.

When it's a family space plants must be **child-friendly**, so choose kinds that don't have spikes, sharp-edged leaves or pointed bits. Avoid bamboos, yucca, berberis and pyracantha, and be wary of anything with berries that small children may be tempted to taste (not many are truly harmful, but it's best not to risk it). Make sure plants aren't irritant or toxic (garden centres often keep a list of poisonous plants so ask, and check the small print on the back of labels, before buying) – ones to avoid in particular are euphorbia, laburnum, aconite and rue.

For ease of maintenance opt for reliable, **easy-going plants**, the more foolproof the better. Do check they suit the growing conditions, or they won't last long. Don't clutter the area with plants, instead use a few **dramatic plants** with architectural shapes and show them off in places they'll look most striking. Moisture-loving plants look good in a raised bed growing close to a water feature. Good kinds include hostas, astilbes and arching stems of Solomon's seal, and all three team up well together and are fine in light shade or full sun (as long as the soil stays damp). For a showy one-off try equisetum – it's a relative of horsetail that likes boggy ground and won't get out of hand in a raised bed. It looks stunning grown in a large clump on its own against a plain-coloured background.

For a **hot, dry and sunny spot**, African lilies (*Agapanthus*) are stunning. Alternatively, go for a bed of **aromatic herb**s or pinks for scent. **Grasses and sedges** are also ideal – grow low, drought-tolerant kinds such as blue fescue or stripy variegated sedges in gravel, between pebbles or in gaps between paving slabs in seating areas. Wispy colourful kinds such as Mexican feather grass are good for containers. Tall miscanthus looks architectural and makes a gentle rustling sound when the wind blows – it's a plant you can listen to, well worth growing when you can't have a water feature for any reason. It's also great for muffling distant traffic noise or muting the sound of conversation.

For a **small-but-striking tree** that makes a great conversation piece, choose shiny barked cherry (*Prunus serrula*), a weeping birch (which small children like to play or hide under) or *Acer griseum*, which has shaggy bark that peels off in strips.

LIGHTING

Garden lighting is a great asset to a garden created for entertaining – it means you can keep the party going without guests feeling it's time they got up and left, and it gives the garden a dramatic new adult look after dark. Most people 'get by' using an ordinary porch light over the back door plus tea lights in jam jars, garden lanterns with candles and oil-filled torches. These look lovely and make a romantic atmosphere, but they don't really pick out the garden.

Solar-powered lights are best used for marking the edges of paths, which helps guests find their way around. These recharge themselves as long as they stand in a place that gets bright light during the day – they'll light up automatically at night, but there's usually an over-ride switch so you can leave them turned off when you choose.

Electric outdoor lighting is perfect for when you want more dramatic lighting that picks out the garden's best features and creates an atmosphere. If money is no object, or you're 'decorating' for a special party, then you can pay a specialist lighting firm to do the job for you – for a price. Otherwise put in your own lighting system – once the basics are in place, it's easy to add more for occasions such as children's parties or Christmas. First install an outdoor power supply – an electrician will put in all-weather outdoor sockets at key places where you'll need them. When choosing lights make sure you go for a low-voltage system, then if you happen to pierce a cable you won't get electrocuted. The cables for garden lights are all waterproof but they need to be buried so they are out of the way – if they are to be buried in a border put them below spade or fork depth, and in a lawn at least 10cm (4in) down. You can then plug in to the power supply box and shut the lid, leaving the cable coming out through a gap.

Use different types of outdoor lights for different jobs, playing around with them at night to discover the most effective places to position them. **Floodlights** are the most powerful, and are best for highlighting a focal point such as a statue or piece of sculpture. Sit the light at ground level and point it up so it shines on the statue at a good angle – it will also light up a bit of the surrounding area, creating interesting shapes and shadows.

Spotlights are quite strong but have a fairly narrow beam. Site one that's not too powerful at the base of an interesting tree and shine the light up the trunk to pick out details such as shiny or peeling bark.

Up-lighters and down-lighters are weaker, and handy for creating pools of light on a wall, or to pick out a plant or group of flowers.

Wall-mounted lights are great in a seating area as they give out enough light for people to see to eat – you can even get waterproof outdoor standard lamps that recreate an outdoor living room feeling.

♣ For the finishing touch, consider adding an outdoor fireplace feature. There are various cast-iron braziers and ceramic chimineas used for burning logs that give off flickering flames and a little warmth. There are also 'designery' contemporary alternatives; one such device looks like a sheaf of stainless steel tubes leaning together in the centre with a reservoir in the middle that takes bio-ethanol – when it's lit it gives a bit of heat and looks very pretty with flames. Any of these make a good alternative to the ubiquitous bottled-gas-powered patio heater.

Make the most of an entertainment garden – build a fire pit

A fire pit makes a stylish alternative to the usual barbecue, and recreates a wonderful feeling of cooking over an open camp fire that brings out your inner boy scout. And when you've finished cooking, you and your guests can snuggle around the dying embers for a bit of extra warmth after dark. A fire pit adds bags of atmosphere, it's also incredibly easy and inexpensive to build. Since it uses real logs instead of charcoal it's cheap to run and quite 'green', especially if logs are grown locally and not transported from overseas – as is usually the case with charcoal.

1. Choose a place with level ground, well away from the house and any overhanging trees or anything else that's inflammable, but not too far from your seating area so guests can watch the cook in action. Make sure there's plenty of room to walk all round the fire pit, and space to put cooking utensils etc.

2. Mark out a circle approximately 1m across, using a length of string with a metal skewer tied at each end. Spike one skewer into the turf where you want the centre of your fire pit, pull the string taut and use the other skewer to 'draw' a circle all around it.

3. Strip off the turf, leaving a circle of bare soil. In the centre of that, dig a neat round hole about 30cm (12in) deep and 45cm (18in) wide with a level base.

4. Put a layer of gravel in the bottom of the hole – this acts as insulation, holding heat when the pit is in use, and helping rainwater to run away quickly when it's not.

5. Place a square of sheet metal, or an old metal camping plate, on top of the gravel (this helps reflect the heat upwards, but also makes the pit easier to clean after use).

6. Stand two heavy concrete building blocks either side of the metal plant, and use them to support an old oven shelf or a proper barbecue grill (from some DIY centres).

7. Remove the grill rack, and build a fire in the bottom of the pit boy-scout-style. Use screwed up newspaper and dry twigs to begin with, progressing to proper logs as the fire gets going. Let the fire burn vigorously for 40 minutes, so it forms a good base of hot embers and big chunks of glowing coals (you don't want lots of big flames).

The fire will by then have reached cooking temperature. Don't add more wood at this stage, instead put the grill rack in place and start cooking the food.

SHOULDER OF LAMB WITH GARDEN HERBS

SERVES: 4–6

Preparation time
1 hour

Ingredients
A whole shoulder of lamb
A few sprigs each of
    oregano, rosemary,
    thyme and some
    fennel tops
10–12 anchovy fillets
2 handfuls of kalamata
    black olives, stoned
1 bulb of garlic, peeled
    and split into cloves
Zest and juice of 1 lemon

The days when you could get away with feeding guests frozen burgers and burnt sausages have long gone. For the perfect summer meal, cook up a shoulder of lamb with herbs you've grown in the garden (plant a selection of favourites in spring and by the barbecue season they'll be ready to use).

Method

1. Score the outside of the lamb quite deeply, so the herbs can 'soak in' during cooking.

2. To make the marinade, strip the herbs off their stems (you need about two handfuls in total) and place on a wooden chopping board. Add the anchovies (the salt content acts as seasoning so you don't need any extra salt, and the fishy taste disappears during cooking), olives, garlic and the lemon zest and juice. Chop the whole lot up together.

3. Rub the herb purée into the lamb, working it into the cuts. Sprinkle chopped rosemary over the top. Wrap the whole thing in tin foil, folding the edges over firmly to make a parcel.

4. Place the parcel of meat in the fire pit, so it sits flat on top of the cooking rack. Leave it for 25 minutes, then turn it over and give it 20 minutes on the other side. Remove, and to serve, pull the meat apart on a large tray in front of your guests – it all adds a sense of 'theatre'. Serve with bowls of salad, crusty bread or jacket potatoes. Yummy!

CHAPTER 8
THE EXOTIC GARDEN

You don't have to go on the holiday of a lifetime to enjoy a Sultan's lifestyle – create an exotic garden at home and turn all your weekends, evenings and time-off into an instant mini break. It's perfectly possible, even if you only have a postage-stamp space in a city centre. Just think 'Arabian Nights' and you won't go far wrong with a few lush-looking plants and some glamorous props, you'll be ready to 'come to the kasbah'.

If you want the ultimate escape, go for the exotic - a formal pool with a fountain at its centre, tiled floors, lanterns and an interesting sculpture. Remember that tender plants will need to be overwintered in a frost-free greenhouse or conservatory.

WHAT MAKES AN EXOTIC GARDEN?

Minarets and Moorish architecture, colourful tiled floors, the splash of fountains and lots of lush foliage all arranged in an enclosed courtyard provide the recipe for this particular exotic look. For inspiration, look at pictures of the series of courtyards and garden 'rooms' at the Alhambra, Grenada, and downsize ideas to suit your space.

Top tip: Choosing decorations

Choose Moroccan-style furniture, furnishings and decorations. Metal lanterns and elaborate white bird-cages are traditional (these look stunning with a flowing leafy plant such as a ladder fern or spider plant stood inside), but all sorts of other knick-knacks, containers and richly coloured cushions add to the effect. Choose good-quality garden furniture that's designed to be left outside all year round, since it saves under-cover storage space and forms part of the scenery.

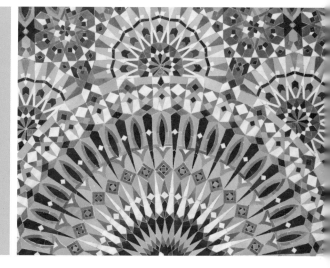

GET THE LOOK

THE DESIGN

The Moorish look is great for a tiny town or city garden, especially a courtyard that's already enclosed by high walls or fences, which provide privacy. It's an inward-looking garden that's meant to be screened off from the outside world, so the emphasis is concentrated on a central feature rather than distant vistas. And since the style originates from hot dry countries, there's no lawn to maintain – it's replaced by tiled flooring, and instead of traditional flower borders there are raised beds around the edges, which in turn means even less routine maintenance. All this makes it a good style for busy people.

Being rather geometrical, this is a very easy type of garden to design and straightforward to draw on squared graph paper. Start with your central, most dominant feature – usually a raised bed or water feature – and work outwards from there, via wide expanses of paving with room for seats and groups of containers, to raised beds around the edge.

Plants are essential for setting the scene – besides a succession of exotic flowers for interest, you'll need lots of foliage to act as screening and provide shade. Props provide lots of fun for decorating in a Moroccan theme – make the most of stylish and unusual containers for showing off a few key plants. A splashy water feature is also a key element of a real Moorish garden, although a large bowl of still water makes a good alternative.

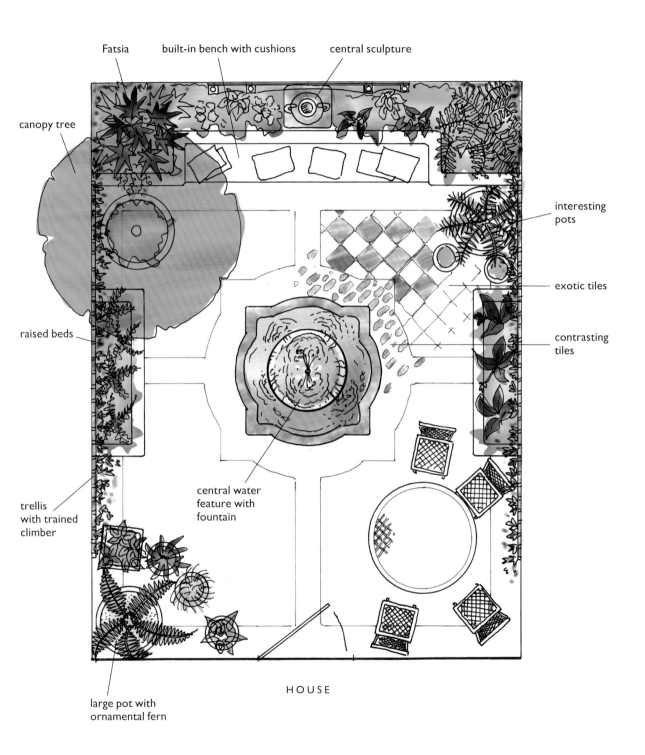

Fatsia

built-in bench with cushions

central sculpture

canopy tree

interesting pots

exotic tiles

contrasting tiles

raised beds

trellis with trained climber

central water feature with fountain

large pot with ornamental fern

HOUSE

Palms will add height and exotic climbers will provide colour in your exotic garden.

THE PLANTS

With a pocket-hanky-sized garden, the temptation is to fill the space with lots of tiny plants, thinking they'll make the garden look bigger, but with this style the reverse is true. Use **big, bold architectural plants** to create an exotic look, but use them well so they seem to expand the space. The trick is to arrange them carefully to provide a series of different heights, so each plant stands out without looking overcrowded.

Real exotic plants aren't hardy in Britain, so cheat and use ones that look exotic because of their large, showy, lush-looking leaves, but which are hardy enough to withstand our winters. In a courtyard enclosed by walls or buildings, especially in or near cities, the microclimate often means temperatures stay slightly higher, so in those situations you can usually get away with growing slightly tender plants that won't survive outside elsewhere.

Good plants for creating an exotic look outside include cabbage palm (*Cordyline*, in green or purple, slightly tender), false castor oil plant (*Fatsia japonica*, tough as old boots almost everywhere), New Zealand flax (*Phormium*, with large strap-shaped leaves, often striped boldly in cream, green and pink or orange), hardy banana (*Musa basjoo*), Chusan palm (*Trachycarpus*) and bamboos.

Train **climbers** over walls and fences to make solid boundaries 'disappear' and give the impression that the surrounding jungle is encroaching on the garden. If you need to mask neighbouring houses and create a more secret interior, use strong trellis panels to add extra height to the top of existing walls. Evergreen climbers give the best year-round effect – go for a mixture of good foliage and showy flowers such as *Clematis armandii* 'Apple Blossom' (architectural leaves and pink flowers), Chilean potato vine (*Solanum crispum*, clusters of blue and yellow 'potato flowers' and very little foliage) and Chilean bellflower (*Lapageria rosea*, tubular pink flowers, tender). Passionflower (*Passiflora caerulea*, big showy blue and white rosette flowers produced over most of the summer, followed by large orange fruits) and *Actinidia kolomikta* (not evergreen, but has showy pink, cream and green leaves in summer) are also good options.

Plant a few **tallish trees with airy foliage** to create a light canopy of leaves overhead – good kinds include acacia (fluffy yellow balls of flower in early spring), azara (marzipan-scented flowers in early spring), tamarix (feathery foliage and tiny pink flowers in summer) and tree of heaven (*Ailanthus altissima*, ferny foliage, potentially huge but much prettier if cut back hard every year or two, which makes the leaves grow even bigger). Although a selection of suitable plants should be available at larger garden centres, especially close to large cities, it may pay to search farther afield. For a wide choice and more unusual varieties, look out for nurseries that specialise in exotic or architectural plants and pay them a visit to see what's available and what goes together.

Top tip: pruning tall trees

To avoid sitting in gloom, lightly thin tree canopies to create delicate dappled shade. Use a long-arm telescopic pruner to avoid teetering around up ladders. This handy device has a long pole-like handle with the secateur blades set in the top, and is operated from ground level either by tugging on a rope or operating a lever. The best time to prune purely foliage trees is in winter when they are dormant. Prune flowering trees such as acacia just after flowering, that way they have time to recover and give you a great display again next year.

Make an exotic raised bed

Raised beds are a good way of incorporating lots of plants around the edges of an exotic courtyard-style garden. Although the centre of a garden like this may be nice and sunny, the backs of beds round the edges can be quite shady – the mistake most people make is planting sun lovers in these shady places (you can tell when you've got it wrong, because plants grow thin weak and spindly, don't flower and eventually die out entirely).

1. Fill raised beds initially with a 50:50 mixture of good topsoil (or use bags of John Innes No. 3 potting compost) and peat-free multipurpose compost. Mix in some water-retaining crystals, since the soil in raised beds can often be rather dry. When replacing plants in existing raised beds, work more multipurpose compost into the gaps where old plants have been removed. (fig. 1)

2. Use good background foliage plants in the shadiest places. Spotted laurel (*Aucuba japonica*) is ideal as it looks fairly tropical with its yellow-spotted evergreen leaves but is brilliant at coping with dry shade and soil. False castor oil plant (*Fatsia japonica*), a large, glossy evergreen with fig-shaped leaves (there's a variegated form which is showier but a tad tender), and some ferns (*Dryopteris*) also do well in slightly drier conditions. (fig. 2)

3. For sunnier spots towards the front of the bed choose exotic flowers and foliage, and some near-hardy house plants. Good kinds include purple-leaved cannas for exotic flowers and foliage (keep the tubers in a frost-free place in winter), tree ferns to create a lacy canopy above a craggy looking trunk, mother-in-law's tongue and pink-flowered calla lilies (arum lily-like; bring the tubers indoors in winter to reuse next year). Mother-in-law's tongue is not hardy in Britain, but cheat – sink the pots in place in the border and pull the plants out to keep indoors in winter. (fig. 3)

4. Edge raised beds with stripy fountains of spider plants and some semperflorens begonias. They'll both die off in the winter, but will soften the hard straight edges of the beds for most of the summer. They don't cost much to replace the following year. (fig. 4)

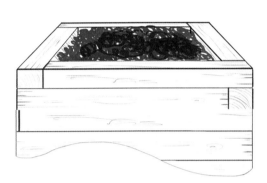

FIG. I

FIG. 2

FIG. 3

FIG. 4

AN EXOTIC PATIO

The right sort of flooring sets the whole tone for this style of garden. Instead of traditional patio-type paving slabs, use smaller semi-shiny tiles perhaps 8–10cm (3–4in) square. Terracotta tiles (like the quarry tiles often used for kitchen floors) are cheaper than coloured versions, so use those as the mainstay of your pattern and save more expensive coloured tiles to make inset patterns to add detail.

Build raised beds economically from concrete walling blocks (one block high is usually enough) then render the sides and paint them a complementary colour or consider covering them with areas of mosaic or tiling for extra interest. Don't worry that it looks 'too much' – it's just right for this look and contrasts very nicely with all the surrounding green plants on walls. It will also create a light, bright, cheery effect in an area that could otherwise be a tad dark and gloomy – especially if you paint surrounding walls white.

Use pots and containers in the courtyard area. Don't dot lots of little plants in different containers around as it just looks spotty and messy – one statuesque plant in a good container makes much more impact. Give it a good position that shows it off well. Good plants include aeonium (deep red rosette-shaped succulents), agave (strikingly shaped blue or green and yellow-striped succulents, but watch out for pointed leaf-tips), echeveria (blue-bodied rosette-shaped succulents) and aloe (symmetrical spiky succulents). These are all tender and need to be brought under cover in winter. For a bushier or leafier look, try aspidistra, lucky bamboo (sold as small pot plants), hardy yucca, cordyline palm, or *Ilex crenata* (a tiny-leaved, non-prickly holly that's very slow growing, and can be finger-pruned or clipped to shape).

WATER FEATURES

Water is a traditional feature of Moorish gardens, seen as a luxury in the dry arid desert environment. A typical courtyard garden would usually contain a central water feature that might be a showy container of still water, or it might have one single narrow fountain jet playing from the centre. Grander gardens might boast a 'canal' with a row of arched fountains as you see at the Alhambra gardens. Features like these also served a useful function as the water lowered the temperature and created humidity, which acted almost as air conditioning.

It's very easy to create something similar in an exotic garden at home, by sitting a large, shiny, ceramic plant container somewhere central. If it has drainage holes, block them by pushing corks into the holes and sealing over them with clear silcon, but ideally choose one that holds water. Stand it on the floor, oasis-like, surrounded by pots of lush leafy plants, raise it up on a plinth, or stand it on a cast aluminium table sprayed the same colour. Then simply fill with water, and it's done.

If you want something slightly fancier you could customise the basic bowl-of-water theme slightly. Float scented candles on the water at night, for fragrance and moving reflections. Place a small solar fountain in the centre to give the surface of the water a small ripple, or use a nozzle to produce a small spray or fine upright fountain (make sure all the water goes back into the container to stop it emptying and the pump running dry). You could improve on this by putting a few drops of rosewater into the water, so the feature generates a pleasant, Arabic-inspired scent.

Sink a pygmy waterlily into the centre of the bowl (at least 23cm/9in deep). These flower all summer and, being small, are perfect for this type of container. They are more delicate than other miniature waterlilies but will be very happy in the shelter of a courtyard as long as they stand in the sun. But they won't enjoy sharing facilities with candles or fountains.

For a really green water feature, set a decorative tank in a convenient place and have it plumbed in so it stores rainwater diverted from the roof of your house, conservatory or shed. Use the contents for watering your raised beds and containers.

SCENTED PLANTS

To give the garden exotic Arabian-nights-style scents, grow plants such as the scented-leaved pelargonium called 'Attar of Roses' (which smells of Turkish delight) and night phlox (an unusual hardy annual with white, star-shaped flowers that open in the evenings and smell like dolly mixtures – you can grow your own from seed). Stand them on a table top close to your favourite evening seat.

For a more powerful fragrance that's strongest at night, buy night-scented jessamine from a conservatory plant specialist. The plant is unspectacular and the flowers aren't showy – just tubular and greenish to off-white – but it can fill a whole courtyard with scent. It can stand outside in summer but needs winter protection, so move it to a conservatory and keep it frost free. If there's wall space, go for star jasmine (*Trachelospermum jasminoides*) – it's a large, slightly tender evergreen climber with strongly jasmine-scented white flowers for 6–8 weeks in mid-summer.

EXOTIC GARDENS UNDER GLASS

A conservatory is the ideal place for an exotic garden, as it allows you to grow showy and spectacular tender plants that wouldn't survive outside. You'll find a good selection in the conservatory section of garden centres and at specialist conservatory plant nurseries.

A good, lush, plant-filled conservatory creates a wonderful winter retreat where you can continue enjoying exotic surroundings when the outdoor garden display comes to an end, and this sort of scheme taps the hidden potential of conservatory space that is often under-used out of season.

Use pots, troughs and hanging baskets to display plants at different levels, and make a tiered display stand against a wall – this could be something as simple as a set of old shelves, a couple of planks stood on concrete blocks or several old wooden apple boxes standing on top of each other. You can also buy smart tiered conservatory units.

Use trailing plants for top shelves. Hearts-on-a-string (ceropegia) is an unusual houseplant with fat, waxy, silver and green heart-shaped leaves and strange flowers dotted along long, thin, thread-like stems. It doesn't need a lot of watering as it's a succulent so you can put it up on a high shelf (or box) and let it trail right down to the floor. Good trailers for a top shelf in light shade include spider plant and mother-of-thousands – in both cases leave all the 'babies' to cascade down from the parent plant at the end of their runners. If the conservatory is heated to roughly room temperature, you can grow the wax plant (*Hoya*) with buds that open into a shower of little waxy pink stars.

Use orchids for a dramatic injection of colour (room temperature is essential for these). Moth orchid (*Phalaenopsis*) is not expensive, the flowers last a long time and the same plants will flower again and again so they are very good value. For maximum impact, group three plants together in a large, deep container, hiding the tops of the pots with a thin layer of moss, which holds moisture and maintains the humidity the plants like. Do the same thing with maidenhair ferns, which always do best when standing in an inch of water.

Grow large, lush, exotic foliage plants like kentia palm in containers stood on the ground. If you are generous with the shapes and the forms it somehow fools the eye into thinking there's more space than there really is – it's an odd design quirk.

♣ The secret of success with conservatory plants is to avoid extremes of temperature. In summer use blinds to cut out strong sun, and either damp the floor down with water to increase the humidity for tropical plants, or stand a few bowls of water on windowsills – make them part of the display. In winter don't let the temperature drop below 10°C – an electric fan heater with a thermostat is the most economical way of heating and also produces dry air which helps to combat fungus diseases.

MAKE THE MOST OF AN EXOTIC GARDEN – GROW YOUR OWN CITRUS FRUIT

Our winters are too cold for citrus plants to grow outside year-round – growing them in pots which are stood temporarily on the patio in summer then moved under cover for the winter, works quite well. Grow the plants in special citrus compost (from garden centres and specialist citrus plant nurseries) and use liquid feeds specifically for citrus plants.

In reality you'll get far more fruit from a citrus tree grown under cover all year round, in a free-standing bed in a conservatory, where its roots have more room to spread out and the plant can reach a reasonable size. A single lemon tree can produce more than 30lbs of fruit per year, grown this way. Fill the bed with a nutrient-rich compost and apply liquid feed once a month. Water carefully – wait till the soil is almost dry then water thoroughly and don't do so again until the soil is just starting to dry out.

Lemons are the most popular and successful fruit to grow in our country as they'll ripen reliably and will carry flowers and fruit at various stages of ripeness at the same time over most of the year. Kumquats are not so well known, and look like tiny, rather odd-shaped oranges with a very bitter/sour taste. You can eat them whole or poach them with sugar and spices, and they are the hardiest of the citruses which can tolerate temperatures down to –5°C so do well with little or no winter heating. Like lemons, they also flower and fruit at the same time for most of the year.

LEMON POSSET
SERVES: 12

Preparation time
10 minutes plus 2 hours
setting time
Not suitable for freezing

Ingredients
1.2 litres double cream
140g caster sugar
Juice and zest of 2 large
   lemons

For the kumquat sauce
2 large handfuls ripe
   kumquats, roughly
   chopped
2 tablespoons sugar

Method

1. Pour the cream and sugar into a saucepan, warm slowly over a medium heat and bring very briefly to the boil.

2. Remove from the heat, add the lemon juice and zest.

3. Whisk for 30 seconds.

4. Pour the mixture into small ramekins – the lemon juice will thicken the cream mixture naturally.

5. Place in the fridge for 2 hours before serving.

For the kumquat sauce

1. Place chopped kumquats and sugar in a saucepan and add just enough water to cover.

2. Gently boil, stirring constantly, until the sugar has dissolved and the juice has reduced to a syrupy consistency.

3. Pour a tablespoon of kumquat sauce over each individual lemon posset to serve.

CHAPTER 9

THE SEASIDE GARDEN

As an island nation, we are never further than 72 miles from the sea (a farm at Coton in the Elms, Derbyshire, is officially the furthest point). The seaside is still our favourite destination for a day out, a weekend break or a family holiday. Most 'trippers' day-dream of their own seaside retreat – even if it's just a beach hut – but for folk who really do live by the sea, conditions can be tricky. Coastal gardens are faced with problems that inlanders don't experience – strong winds, blown sand and salt spray create a difficult environment that many plants can't tolerate. Seaside sunlight is very intense during the summer months as it's reflected off the water, and it's not just holidaymakers who suffer from sunburn, a lot of delicate plants do too. There's an upside, naturally – the surroundings offer an opportunity for creating something special using seaside elements. The same features can be used inland to create a garden with a seaside flavour that makes every day a holiday. Doubly so, since it's naturally low-maintenance.

You can be on holiday every day of the year with a seaside garden, even if you are miles from the coast!

WHAT MAKES A SEASIDE GARDEN?

The cries of the gulls, the rhythmic swish of waves on the shore, the bracing air and bright light tell you instantly you're by the seaside. Nautical props help to enhance the scene – even with inland gardens – so choose any combination of ropes, chains, pebbles, sand, shells and chunks of driftwood. Distressed timbers, an anchor, a brightly painted beach hut plus a few carefully chosen plants also set the seaside scene.

Top tip: sun lovers

Due to the exceptionally bright light close to the coast, seaside gardens are the best place to grow plants whose flowers only open when the sun shines on them. These include osteospermum, gazania, star of the veldt (*Dimorphotheca*), and the semi-succulent lampranthus, portulaca and Livingstone daisy (*Mesembryanthemum*). These are usually treated as annuals, or tender perennials, but in mild seaside locations some will survive most winters outside.

GET THE LOOK

THE DESIGN

The secret of a successful garden close to the coast lies in creating shelter to protect plants from the elements, without totally obliterating valuable sea views. It's best done by creating a shelter-belt using salt- and wind-tolerant plants to screen the part of the garden that faces the sea (good plants for this difficult situation include tamarisk, escallonia, *Cupressus macrocarpa* and Leyland cypress). Leave 'peepholes' in the plants so you can still see out through gaps. Some people use an old wooden window frame set up in a hole carved through a hedge, or they'll make a gateway for their own access down to the beach (slatted wood or railings are best as you can still see through when the gate is closed).

Many seaside gardeners leave their plots wide open, laying them out with very few plants and a lot of seaside features. All that's needed then is a strong, glass-fronted balcony or veranda along the back of the house where they can sit in comfort – screened from the wind and spray, the horizon-wide sea views can be enjoyed in all weathers.

For folk who live a little further back from the sea, it's worth taking stronger measures to shelter the garden. Fence and delicate trellis or bamboo screens don't last long in windy situations like this, and even walls don't 'work', as the wind somersaults over the top creating strong eddies that can do even more damage. The answer is to slow the wind down instead of trying to stop it entirely. Plants make natural 'wind filters', so create denser shelter belts from a mixture of seaside-tolerant shrubs to protect the garden, then grow choicer ingredients safe inside the heart of the garden. If the situation has free-draining ground, a semi-sunken seating area makes a natural escape from the breeze.

railway sleeper steps

nautical knick-knacks

compost bin

water butt

beach hut

sculpture
(made from
pebbles,
rope etc.)

driftwood
posts

sloping lawn
(arrow pointing upwards)

HOUSE

THE SEA!

glass fronted

shelter-belt
hedge

decking

gap in hedge
with window
frame

steps

nautical
knick-knacks

railway sleeper steps

mixed planting

palms

sheltered sunken
garden with gravel

If you really do have a garden by the sea, choose plants that can cope with salt-laden winds.

THE PLANTS

Only **the toughest plants** tolerate conditions very close to the beach, although our coastal natives are a good place to start. Horned poppy has rugged leaves, sea kale is positively rubbery with grey-blue leaves and clouds of frothy white flowers, sea holly has spiky silvery-blue-green foliage and matching slightly metallic-looking flowers, and sea pinks (thrift) have tufts of linear leaves and tight-packed pink flowers. All four are pretty enough to grow in gardens right up to the sea's edge, accompanied by tamarisk bushes or a double-flowered gorse.

Other good plants you'll often see thriving in coastal gardens include the erigeron daisy (which makes large, low, spreading carpets covered with pink, mauve-ish or purple flowers all summer), silvery-leaved senecio (*Brachyglottis* 'Sunshine') and sea lavender (a colourful cultivated cousin of a wild seaside perennial). Hardy fuchsias, pittosporum, euonymus and the sort of hebes with long, narrow leaves and bottlebrush flowers also do well. Hydrangeas, surprisingly, thrive in gardens a few rows of houses back from the sea, where there's some protection, too.

A little further away from the sea, but within two miles of it, there's often a **mild micro-climate** where relatively tender plants can be cultivated very successfully. You may see south-coast gardens with plants such as bottlebrush (*Callistemon*) thriving, and areas such as the Isle of Wight, Devon, Cornwall, Dorset, the Isles of Scilly and the Channel Islands are well known for their **exotic subtropical planting** schemes. These include relatively **hardy palms, yuccas and nearly-hardy succulents** such as lampranthus. Coasts further north are usually far too cold in winter for such luxuries, so be sure to look around and see what grows well in other gardens in the area. Also ask for advice at your garden centre before buying.

When you're making a seaside-style garden inland, where conditions are kinder, look for **plants that suggest the seaside** without worrying about whether they'd survive there for real. Create seaweedy shapes using groups of grasses or sedges (curly varieties are specially successful) and use mallows and ornamental sea hollies in borders. Include lots of **sun lovers**, such as gazania and pelargoniums in pots, and grow drought-proof plants in gravel and pebbles.

CHOICE SHRUBS

One of the joys of visiting the seaside, for a garden-lover, is spotting unfamiliar plants you rarely see anywhere else. Here are my top choices:

Tamarix Large deciduous shrubs or small trees with flaking bark, feathery foliage and masses of tiny, pink, fluffy flowers arranged in short spikes near the tips of the branches. It flowers in early or late summer, depending on the variety, and is grown as a windbreak or free-standing specimen.

Griselinia (*Griselinia littoralis*) A dense, evergreen shrub with large, thick and oval waxy-textured leaves. It's often used as a hedge or shelter belt on mild coasts. Variegated forms are showier but a tad more tender.

Sea buckthorn (*Hippophae rhamnoides*) A large, spiny, silver-grey shrub with narrow needle-like leaves and large clusters of orange berries near the tips of the shoots in late summer and autumn. It's often grown as a windbreak.

Duke of Argyll's tea tree (*Lycium barbarum*) A quite unusual, upright deciduous shrub with narrow leaves. It has pale purplish-blue, nodding, funnel-shaped flowers and is happy growing in sandy soil. It provides food for the caterpillars of the rare death's head hawk-moth.

NAUTICAL KNICK-KNACKS

Nautical knick-knacks are a lot of fun, and an easy way to give a garden instant seaside style. You can find your own beachcomber booty on the beach, between the high and low water marks. It's okay to pick up shells, the clusters of old egg cases known as 'mermaid's purses' and bits of seaweed, but the removal of pebbles is prohibited as they form a valuable part of sea defences. Anything you find in the way of driftwood, floats, bits of net or rope, ancient life rings and other flotsam and jetsam are fair game, but you should notify the coastguard of anything valuable which has washed up from a shipwreck (it's their job to find the real owner). You can also find interesting coastal curiosities by trawling antique markets, surfing the Internet or by visiting a garden centre or florists near the coast. Here are a few ideas to get you started:

A short stretch of breakwater or section of jetty is easily recreated using some rough timber nailed to upright posts. Alternatively, just use a few very rugged weathered posts to give a suggestion of features half-swallowed by the sea.

Some coastal garden centres sell beach-hut-style sheds and summerhouses, although it's easy to customise an existing shed. Paint it gaily in blue and white, and perhaps add a bit of decking and a short length of timber pergola outside the door to make a beach-hut-style porch.

Buy real canvas folding deckchairs, furniture made from faux driftwood or perhaps a canopied daybed surrounded by wispy voile curtains that billow in the breeze.

Add decorative touches around the garden wherever they're needed (they'll look best grouped with seaside-style plants. Try a rusty iron lobster, a few glass fisherman's floats grouped with some old netting on a bed of pebbles, or an anchor with a length of chain attached. A shoal of painted wooden fish-on-sticks teams well with an evergreen plant.

Make a weathervane from a flattish piece of driftwood whittled roughly into the shape of a ship or fish as the vane.

Thread together small pieces of gnarled driftwood or shells to make 'necklaces' to hang on a wall or drape over a big stone.

Make papier-mache seagulls or other themed shapes on canes to stand in key positions – apply several coats of marine varnish. They won't last more than a year or two, but it's fun to make new ones, and a great summer holiday project for children.

Make a look-out point

If you have an area of accessible flat roof, perhaps on a garage, transform it into a grand look-out point where you can enjoy the view. Before converting a bit of flat roof, consult your local authority as you may need planning permission, and be aware of structural limitations since flat roofs aren't usually designed to take a lot of weight.

1. Use painted trellis screwed to the wall to hide the brickwork, and lay decking squares (which have a natural seaside air about them) on wooden 'rafters' of four-by-two over the floor space. The 'rafters' hold the decking squares steady and can be fixed to the edge of the roof for extra stability.

2. Twist chandler's rope through the uprights to give plain wooden railings a nautical feel.

3. Add nautical knick knacks – perhaps a little wall-mounted cupboard made from driftwood for essentials such as suntan lotion, plus a couple of old-fashioned canvas deckchairs. Hang up a bit of old rope ladder, a bit of mirror with a driftwood frame and drape some old nautical-looking bunting round the walls.

4. Use a few pots of seaside-friendly plants in the most sheltered spot (use soil-less compost and plastic containers to keep the weight down). Good plants include Chusan palm (*Trachycarpus*), African lily (*Agapanthus*), African daisy (*Osteospermum*), echeveria, gazania, erinus, pelargoniums and thrift.

Create a weathered structure

A weathered timber obelisk with a rope spiraling around it gives the garden a nautical feel, and looks great standing in a busy flowerbed. Grow climbers up it, or leave it bare to create contrasts with a sea of plants at its feet. Use chandler's rope, a doorknob for the finial on top and ordinary timber from a DIY store or builders' merchant.

1. Cut four 120cm (4ft) lengths of 40mm x 4mm timber. Cut a semi-circular notch 50mm (2in) from the end of two of the lengths (this is to secure the rope later, so make the notch a suitable diameter). (fig. 1)

2. Next, make four tapered panels that will form the box at the base of the obelisk. Select twelve 3mm x 20cm planks, and cut them to the width you want your obelisk to be. Lay three pieces of plank on a bench parallel to each other a pencil width apart. Take two of the long uprights and lay them on top of the planks, allowing a 25mm (1in) overhang at the base. Make the tops meet to form an apex which will be the top of the pyramid. Using a pencil, draw along the outer edge of each upright to mark a cutting line on the planks. Saw along this. (fig. 2)

3. Fix one end of the planks by screwing a 20mm x 20mm batten flush to the edge of them. Do this four times, screwing batten to plank to create four side panels. Screw the four uprights into each corner of the base. Allow around 25mm (1in) of each upright to poke out of the bottom, creating short legs (which avoids rotting later). (fig. 3)

4. Secure the uprights together by attaching a thin 80mm x 80mm (3in x 3in) square slice of wood where they meet. This will act as a cap to hold them all in place. Make a pilot hole in the centre of the cap and screw the finial in place. (fig. 4)

5. Push the end of the rope into the hole formed by the two notches at the top of the uprights, and anchor it with a screw. Bind both ends of the rope tightly with thin string to stop them fraying. (fig. 5)

6. Spiral the rest of the rope evenly down round the pyramid. Hide the end inside the base and fix it firmly with a screw. Stand the finished obelisk in position and place a potted ornamental grass or sedge in the hollow box at the base. (fig. 6)

> ### Top tip: savvy buying
>
> Look for the word '*littoralis*' in Latin plant names when buying – it means 'of the sea-shore' and means the plant will do well in coastal situations.

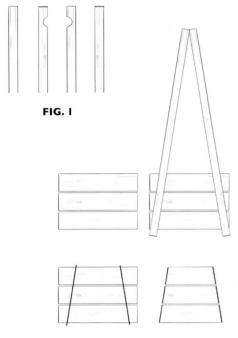

FIG. I

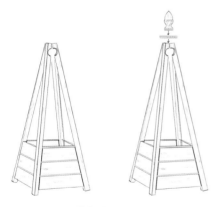

FIG. 2

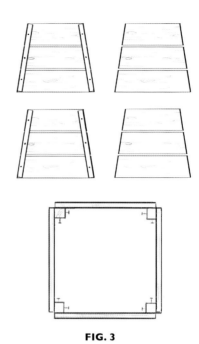

FIG. 3

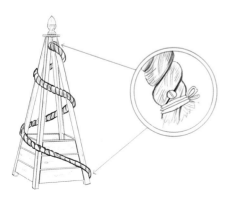

FIG. 4

FIG. 5

FIG. 6

SEASIDE BALCONIES

Since it uses very few plants with just a sprinkling of props, 'seaside' is a very good look to create on balcony outside a flat (regardless of whether it has a real sea-view). Seaside plants are brilliant at coping with the same harsh, windy and bright-sunny conditions often met with in balconies high up. Look for silvery and/or felty leaves such as santolina, lavender, rock rose (*Helianthemum*) and *Convolvulus cneorum* (a small silver-leaved evergreen with white flowers). Snow-in-summer (cerastium, a rock plant with white flowers and silver leaves much despised on rockeries inland since it spreads) is brilliant for tubs or troughs. Plants with naturally thick, waxy or linear leave, including carex sedges, thrift and some semi-succulent rock plants (such as sedums and houseleeks), also thrive, and being hardy can stay outside all year round. For summer-only plant displays good choices include pelargonium, echeveria, gazania and osteospermum.

Group plants together at different heights to create a tiered effect. Either put some on upturned pots to raise them up, or use naturally taller plants such as a standard olive tree or pittosporum to create a top storey to a display. Arrange a 'cameo' using sempervivums planted in large shells, dish-shaped stones or hollow-topped bricks to stand on top of a small table standing against the back wall of the balcony.

Sprinkle a few beach-themed decorations round the balcony – perhaps a driftwood sculpture or a ring of little bits of driftwood hung on the wall. The authentic seaside touches create a relaxing place to sit and watch what's going on, without a lot of upkeep.

MAKE THE MOST OF A SEASIDE GARDEN – CREATE AN OASIS FOR WILDLIFE

A seaside garden might not seem like the natural environment for wildlife, but the coast is the first port of call for migrating birds and butterflies, who are often desperate for rest, food and water after a long sea crossing. But all the 'usual' garden wildlife will also drop in to a seaside haven, so it's worth providing a hedge or some dense banks of shrubs for shelter and a pond for visitors such as frogs, toads, newts, damsel flies and dragonflies. It's been estimated that we have lost 70 per cent of the natural ponds that were once found in our countryside, so even a small one at home helps wildlife immensely.

A good wildlife pond needs plenty of plants. Include a mixture of all the three basic types (oxygenating, waterside and floating), and build the pond with shallow sloping sides so that wildlife can get in and out easily. Oxygenating weeds are the pond's air-conditioning system, and they make a wonderful nest-bed for newts and frogs, tadpoles and tinier pond life. The best oxygenating plant for a small pond is hornwort. Waterside plants round the margins make safe hiding places for various wildlife, and plants with tall, straight upright stems (such as reeds and water irises) are vital for larvae of damsel flies and dragonfly to crawl up while they open out their wings to dry for the first time (the adults only lay their eggs where there are suitable plants for their offspring). Floating plants provide shade and a place for pond snails to lay eggs. The eggs are jelly-like blobs and provide food for all sorts of water wildlife.

If there's no room for a wildlife pond, turn a container (such as a half-barrel made of untreated wood) into a potted pond. Put a couple of bricks in the bottom, then fill it with water (rainwater if possible). Stand some water plants in place round the sides with a little hornwort and a pygmy water lily (the very smallest-growing sort). Lastly, slant a strong stick into the water as a 'bridge' leading to dry land, so that baby frogs etc can get out (a nice gnarled bit looks quite good too). Don't use treated timber – leave it natural and strip off any bark.

CHAPTER 10

THE ROSE GARDEN

Grown here since medieval times, the rose is still Britain's favourite flower and goes hand-in-hand with romance. Roses are famous for their fragrance, colours and exceptionally long flowering season, which is four or five months from early summer well into autumn. They are no longer the preserve of parks departments, stately gardens or chocolate boxes, and today there are more than 3,500 different varieties of rose to choose from. More are on the way too, as breeders strive to produce more compact, disease-free and fragrant varieties. There's a rose to suit every part of today's modern garden, from pots to pergolas and borders and hedges.

The rose is still the nation's favourite flower and it's easy to see why: a wide range of colours, heavenly perfume and the ability to either cover the ground, form a self-supporting bush, climb up a wall or mask an ugly shed are all within the rose's capabilities.

WHAT MAKES A ROSE GARDEN?

It sounds obvious, but wall-to-wall roses are the hallmark of a great rose garden. If the scent doesn't bowl you over first, you'll be staggered by the sight of roses banked up in beds and borders, growing up the walls, along pergolas, over arches, fences, structures and outbuildings, up through trees and even filling tubs on the patio. It's a symphony of colour and scent. But setting off all those roses will be a supporting cast of tall perennials forming a top tier, with an under-storey of low carpeters. For out of season interest there'll also be spring bulbs and a framework of evergreens. It looks spectacular, but anyone can create a rose lover's paradise, even in a small space.

Top tip: new climbers

Spread the stems of new climbers and ramblers out and tie them in place so the plant covers all the space evenly as it grows. Keep tying in new main stems till you've filled all the space. When growing a climber or rambler up a pillar or post, spiral it round the support – this encourages flowers to form all the way up, not just at the top.

GET THE LOOK

CHOOSING THE RIGHT ROSE

There are several categories of roses in a huge range of shapes and sizes – they're all suited to different places in the garden. Before buying check out the size of the particular variety on the small print on the back of the label. This way you don't end up with a rose that outgrows its welcome or needs more work than you're prepared for.

Bush roses are the traditional hybrid teas and floribundas, once grown in formal rose beds with bare soil underneath, but now far more likely to be found in mixed borders. They need quite hard annual pruning.

Shrub roses are a more easy-going group of roses, needing little or no proper pruning – use them in mixed borders in the same way as any flowering shrub. Some shrub roses make good flowering hedges, with the bonus of spikes to deter intruders. For sheer flower-power look for a group of modern shrub roses known as 'English roses'. Bred by David Austin, they are repeat-flowering with charming 'old-fashioned' flowers that are often exceptionally well scented.

Old-fashioned roses are genuine old varieties, mostly bred in Victorian times and sometimes far earlier – some are now rather rare. They have lots of character, but most only flower once a year (usually for 4–6 weeks at the start of summer). Many have long, leggy stems that need lots of support, so, for all but serious fans, the English roses have largely superseded them.

Patio roses are less than knee high, and especially bred to do well in large tubs. Use soil-based John Innes No. 3 potting compost, water regularly, feed them every week or two through summer with liquid rose food and they'll flower their socks off for months. They make a great alternative to traditional bedding plants for people wanting to avoid replanting containers every season. Patio roses can stay in the same tub for two or three years before they need repotting and require very little pruning.

Miniature roses are the very small ones often sold at petrol stations and greengrocers' shops as indoor pot plants. They are actually outdoor plants best grown in raised beds in a sheltered spot, or a trough on a patio or windowsill. Snip off dead flowerheads in summer, and remove any dead ends of shoots in late spring.

Ground-cover roses are another modern innovation in rose breeding. These low-growing varieties are intended for the front of a border but they're also brilliant for growing over a 'problem' bank where mowing grass is difficult or dangerous. Some varieties form neat, low, mound shapes, while others have longish stems that grow prostrate along the ground. One or two are even suitable for growing in hanging baskets, though you'd need to be lavish with feeding and watering.

Standard roses are simply bush roses that have been grafted onto short stems so they make miniature tree-shapes. Once used to give height to a formal rose bed, they are now mostly used in a normal mixed border or grown in a tub on the patio. When a ground-cover rose such as 'Nozomi' is grafted onto a stem, the result is a spectacular weeping rose that looks like a waterfall of flowers.

Species roses are the sort people think of as 'wild' and indeed many are wild plants in other countries. Many are enormous spiky shrubs that only flower once each summer, but some have longer flowering seasons and many are grown for their striking hips. A few species make superb hedges for exposed places as they withstand poor soil and exposed situations, bear both flowers and hips simultaneously and don't grow too big (around 1m/3ft). Choose varieties of *Rosa rugosa* for a 'bit of everything'.

Climbing and rambling roses are the largest of all. They're used for growing on walls, fences and trellis, over arches, pergolas or outbuildings and up through trees. Roses need tying in place, since they can't cling on – in the wilds they use their long-hooked thorns to scramble over other plants. Compact modern varieties are useful for training on pillars or obelisks to add height to a flower border.

GROWING KNOW-HOW

Roses are supposed to prefer clay soil, but they'll grow happily in almost anything – even 'difficult' sand or stony chalk – if you work in lots of well-rotted compost or manure before planting. This, plus generous mulching each spring with more compost or manure, means the roots stay moist, resulting in more flowers and less mildew – a common disease of roses.

Sprinkle rose fertiliser around each rose in March and again in June, to keep them growing and flowering well all season. It's quite okay to use the same rose feed for other flowers growing in the same bed with roses – it saves buying two different products, and other shrubs and flowers appreciate the extra magnesium and potash found in rose food. Don't spray roses unless it's really essential (and even then use something organic), as it's far better to leave greenfly for blue tits and beneficial insects to clear up. If diseases such as blackspot or mildew are a regular problem, replace the affected roses with disease-free varieties and make sure the ground is encouraged to hold on to moisture.

Keep rose bushes looking their best by cutting off the flowers as soon as they fade. You can either snip off individual blooms when one or two among a cluster have 'gone over', or wait till the whole head is finished then cut off the entire stem about 20cm (8in) below the flowers. Always cut just above a leaf, since that encourages a new flowering shoot to grow out quickly from that part of the stem. It's the secret of keeping roses flowering well all summer, and just about all the pruning shrub roses need.

Left to right: top: **bush rose** *Rosa* **'Iceberg'; shrub rose** *Rosa* **'Scharlachglut'; old-fashioned rose** *Rosa gallica* **'Versicolor';** *middle:* **patio rose** *Rosa* **'Free as Air'; miniature rose** *Rosa* **'Wee Jock'; ground-cover rose** *Rosa* **Essex 'Paulnoz';** *bottom:* **standard rose** *Rosa* **'Mary Rose'; species rose** *Rosa glauca* **syn.** *Rosa rubrifolla;* **climbing rose** *Rosa* **'Félicité Perpétue'**

MODERN WAYS TO GROW ROSES

A garden composed solely of roses can look a little boring, so grow other things between them for extra interest. Delphiniums are good with roses – yellow 'Graham Thomas' works well with blue delphinium, rich pink 'Gertrude Jekyll' looks great with purple delphiniums and pale pink 'Abraham Darby' is good with white delphiniums. Other tall perennials to grow among roses include *Verbena bonariensis* (which has tall, bare, green, wiry stems topped by airy blobs of purple flower), and cultivated foxgloves with tall spires of spotted bell-flowers in shades of mauve, pink or cream. For short plants to carpet the ground choose heucheras (with pink, mauve or purplish foliage), hardy cranesbills, variegated brunnera and silver, felty-leaved stachys. Underplant everything with spring bulbs, and early flowers such as forget-me-nots, so the season gets off to an early start. Also include late perennials such as phlox, perennial asters (modern Michaelmas daisies) and Japanese anemones for autumn.

Climbers and rambler roses are traditionally trained flat up against a fence or wall, with their permanent structure of main stems tied to trellis or horizontal wires held up by wall nails. If you like a more modern effect, look out for contemporary trellis, which is available in various modern styles including unusual black metal honeycomb shapes. When climbers and rambler roses are grown on structures such as pergolas or up over arches, the stems need tying in place on the uprights, but once the reach the top they can be allowed to 'wander around' at will. Grow compact modern climbers and rambling roses up pillars or obelisks to give height to a flower border, and tie them in place to keep the distinctive shape.

To create the spectacular tiered wall-of-roses effect, arrange different types of roses of graded heights from the back to the front of borders. Start with climbers and ramblers on the boundaries and growing up through trees. Use tall bush roses or standard roses towards the back of the border, graduating down through more compact modern shrub roses to low ground-cover roses at the front. This way you'll pack lots of roses into the space, yet each one will still stand out as an individual.

Rose pruning explained

Rose pruning is the one thing people worry about, but it's not difficult. Each group of roses needs different pruning, so read the small print on the back of the label when you buy a new rose for detailed instructions. Alternatively, look up the name in a plant encyclopedia or rose-growing guide.

Compact modern climbers and ramblers, and modern shrub roses, need nothing more than regular deadheading during the summer. Tidy up the shape a little if needed when flowering is entirely over for the year and tie in the stems of climbers. Remove a few older stems each year to avoid overcrowding.

Hybrid teas need hard pruning each spring between January and mid-March. Cut these back to about 30cm (12in) above ground level, removing any weak or diseased stems and one or two older ones to leave a cup-shaped framework of vigorous shoots. Always cut just above an outward-facing bud to encourage the cup shape. Floribundas can be pruned in the same way, but not quite so low (to around 45cm/18in). Patio roses need a good 'haircut' to keep them neat and flowering freely, so cut them back to around 15cm (6in).

Standard roses need careful pruning as it's vital not to cut the bushy top off entirely. If the variety grafted on top of the 'trunk' is a hybrid tea or floribunda, prune them back in March to 10–15cm (4–6in) of the main trunk. If it's a ground-cover rose (such as 'Nozomi'), a light tidy up is enough.

Traditional climbers and ramblers are often large plants. Leave a main framework of thick older stems firmly tied up to supports, and remove dead heads regularly. When flowering is entirely over for the year, tie in some of that summer's long shoots to extend the plant's territory and to replace a few of the older stems. Reduce the length of sideshoots to around 15cm (6in).

Species roses shouldn't be pruned until spring, when the display of hips is over. Just tidy the shape of the plants (occasionally you may need to take out an entire old branch that's not flowering well any more) but never cut the plants down hard. Ground-cover roses just need deadheading all summer and a light tidy-up in March, although it's not essential to touch them at all.

COMPACT MODERN CLIMBERS AND RAMBLERS

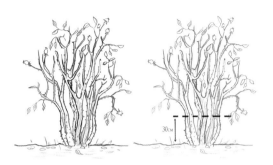

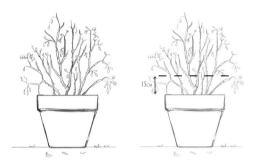

HYBRID TEAS

PATIO ROSES

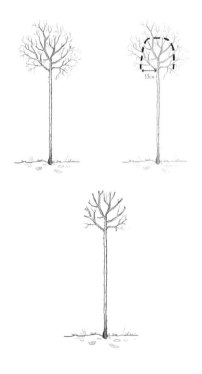

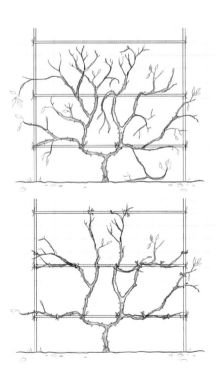

STANDARD ROSES

**TRADITIONAL CLIMBERS
AND RAMBLERS**

Make a rose arch

A dramatic rose-clad archway makes a stunning entrance to a small enclosed garden-within-a-garden. You can make your own arch from rustic poles, but most people buy an inexpensive one in kit form from a garden centre.

1. Open the pack and lay the parts out on the lawn. The arch itself may be adjustable to suit the size of the space available. To work out the right width, lay the two ends of the arching top flat on the grass at the top of the path, then push the ends in or stretch them slightly apart so the arched top is exactly the same width as the path.

2. Push the sides of the arch down into the soil (use a spirit level to make sure the tops are level) and slot the arched centrepiece in place over them.

3. Plant a climbing rose on the outside of the arch so you don't snag your clothes on the thorny stems when you walk underneath (even roses described as 'thornless' may have a few thorns, so don't take chances).

4. Dig the planting hole slightly deeper and wider than the pot your rose is growing in, and work plenty of well-rotted compost or manure into the base. Sprinkle one scoop-full of beneficial root fungi over the base of the planting hole. Don't mix it in as it needs to be in contact with the rose's roots.

5. Lift the rose out of its pot, although don't tease out the roots. Sit it straight into the planting hole. Roses need to be planted a few inches deeper in the ground than they were growing in their pots, so that the bottoms of the stems can take root – this helps them grow more strongly.

6. Train the rose up and over the arch, tying the stems loosely in place with soft twine. Plant perennials around the bottom of the arch to help it blend in – use medium and low plants to lead the eye naturally up to the arch. The shape of the arch makes a great contrast with tall flowers beyond it, which helps it all stand out more sharply (like twiddling the focus knob on your camera).

Make the most of a rose garden – use roses for cooking

Roses aren't just eye candy, they can taste good too and they can be used in all sorts of imaginative ways.

Rose ice cubes

These look lovely, and as they melt the rose petal inside escapes and adds a little gentle fragrance and flavour to your drink. Simply pick off the individual petals of a bright-coloured bloom, making sure they are clean and don't contain any dust or insects.

Also snip off the green base of the petal as this tastes bitter. Place one petal in the bottom of each cell of an ice-cube tray, then fill with water and put in the freezer.

Top tip: perfect partners

Combine roses with clematis to increase the flower power and fill in gaps in the flowering season with other blooms.

Crystallised rose petals

These make great edible decorations to go on top of cakes or ice creams, and they are also good mixed up with meringues. Take individual rose petals (again, use varieties with bright colours and strong scent, and snip off the green bit at the base). Paint each side of the petals with beaten egg white, making sure it's completely covered, then sprinkle all over with caster sugar on both sides. Space the petals out flat on a piece of baking parchment to dry – this takes several days in a warm, dry place such as the airing cupboard. When 'done', store the petals in an airtight jar out of light. They are crispy and sugary, with an intense rose flavour – you could almost eat them as sweets.

ROSEWATER

Rosewater has all sorts of cosmetic uses. You can sprinkle a few drops on your pillow at night to help you relax and get to sleep, or use it to spritz your face. It's also an exquisite food flavouring which can be used in anything from oriental cookery to cup cakes. Although rosewater is commercially produced by a large-scale distillation process, it's a doddle to do on a small scale at home if you boil the petals down, collect the scented steam and bottle it.

Method

1. Pick fully open flowers of a heavily scented variety of rose (the commercial flower-farmer we visited uses an English rose called 'Miranda', whose flowers are made up of lots of petals). Pick the petals off the flowerhead and discard the hard base of the bloom along with any stem.

2. Take a heavy pan with a lid and put a clean fist-sized flat stone in the bottom. Put the petals in the pan around the stone, in a layer about 5cm (2in) deep.

3. Take a heatproof oven dish small enough to fit inside the pan with a gap round the edge, and sit it on the stone.

4. Pour enough water into the bottom of the pan to cover the petals but leave the oven dish empty. Turn the heat on and bring the water to a rolling boil.

5. Cover the pan with its normal lid but turn it upside down – unscrew the central knob that forms its handle and replace it on the other side of the lid, so that when the steam rises it meets the domed lid and drips down from its lowest point in the centre and into the oven dish. Sit a bag of ice on top of the pan lid to help speed up the condensation process.

6. Continue to boil gently for 40 minutes to extract all the scented essential oil from the petals, and leave it in the oven dish as rosewater. When cool, put it in a pretty bottle, and cork firmly or screw the top on.

HARISSA PASTE
SERVES: 12

Preparation time
20 minutes

The strong-flavoured recipe is great with barbecued lamb, chicken or a Moroccan tagine.

Ingredients
12 large red chillies
1 clove garlic
1 teaspoon each of whole
   coriander seeds, cumin
   seeds and caraway seeds
½ teaspoon whole black
   peppercorns
1 teaspoon flaked sea salt
1½ teaspoon tomato paste
1 tablespoon olive oil
Juice of ½ lemon
1 teaspoon rosewater

Method
1. Place the chillies under a very hot grill for 2 minutes each side, until they are turning brown and blistering slightly.

2. Remove the skins, stalks and seeds from the chillies and chop the flesh finely.

3. Chop the clove of garlic and combine with the chilli flesh.

4. Gently toast the coriander, cumin and caraway seeds in a dry pan over a low heat until you can smell toasting spices.

5. Place the toasted seeds in a mortar with the black pepper and salt, and grind together with a pestle into a fine powder.

6. Put the chopped chilli flesh, garlic and ground spice mixture in a bowl, add the tomato paste, olive oil, lemon juice and rosewater, mix, and leave to stand for 20 minutes to infuse before serving.

THE SECRET GARDEN

When you want a retreat from the real world – a place you can retire to after work and just pull up the drawbridge to 'switch off' completely – consider creating your very own secret garden. Subtle planting schemes and clever designer tips can transform the smallest space into a private sanctuary, and the unlikeliest places (such as a badly overlooked area or a dingy passageway outside a basement) can successfully be given the secret-garden treatment. A secluded hideaway is the perfect place to meditate, sunbathe or to install a hot tub and enjoy your own private spa experience. And when you're surrounded by city bustle it makes a haven of peace and quiet in which to sit and read, enjoy a glass of wine or simply do nothing. Well, a man needs a hobby.

There are times when we all want to be alone! A secret garden is a sanctuary; a place to escape the pressures of everyday life. Make sure you have somewhere dry – and comfortable – to sit in a shower of rain or the heat of the summer sun.

WHAT MAKES A SECRET GARDEN?

Clearly the first essential of a secret garden is it must be secretive. Passers by should be able to walk down the street outside without having an inkling of the glories that lie out of sight perhaps only a few feet away. High walls, fences and hedges, along with climber-clad trellis and screens, help keep the world out. To keep the interest in there'll be beautiful planting, subtle decorations, and facilities for relaxing in style and comfort. Its entire ethos is a quiet contemplative atmosphere. Naturally, hard work is kept to the absolute minimum, so no expense is spared to keep the garden ticking over nicely with only minimal intervention. Just switch your mobile phone off, and enjoy.

GET THE LOOK

THE DESIGN

A successful secret garden needs to be enclosed, facing inwards and not out. Existing boundaries may need building up a foot or two – if so, add trellis panels to create sufficient seclusion. Fill gaps in external boundaries with screens of evergreen shrubs or bamboos, or grow climbers over structures, architectural objects or old tree stumps – ivies are fast, look good (especially variegated kinds) and add a faint air of mystery. And make full use of awnings, a pergola or a plant-clad arch to plug a gap in the skyline or screen a view of a neighbouring window (if you can see up to a window, it's reasonable to assume anyone looking out of it can see you).

Avoid falling into the trap of planting too many big, dark-green gloomy evergreens – they'll make a small space seem dark and oppressive. Some quite surprising plants can be used in unusual ways to provide light screening that still gives some privacy. Plant a narrow border of tall lilies – they make a colourful 'divider' inside a garden that's ideal for screening the seating area off from the neighbours. What's more, lilies look very exotic but they're very easy to grow.

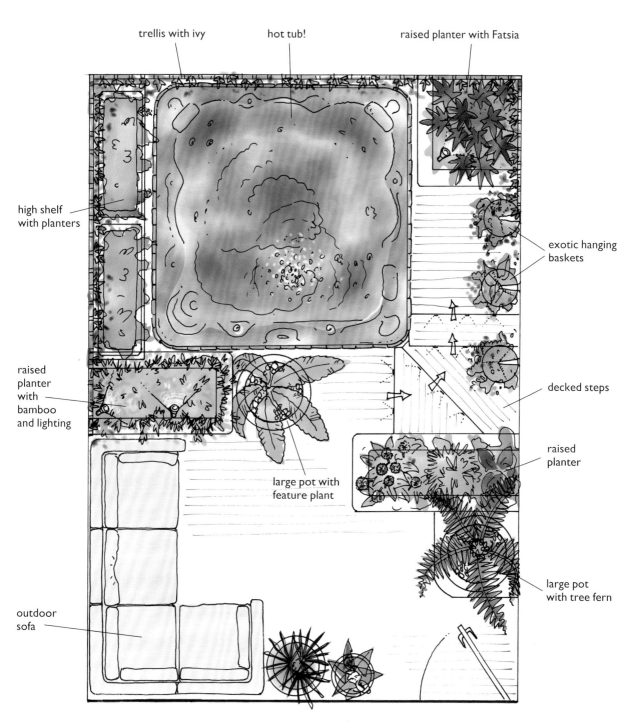

trellis with ivy

hot tub!

raised planter with Fatsia

high shelf
with planters

exotic hanging
baskets

raised
planter
with
bamboo
and lighting

decked steps

raised
planter

large pot with
feature plant

large pot
with tree fern

outdoor
sofa

HOUSE

THE PLANTS

The important thing is to retain an air of mystery. Plants that can create barriers behind which you are tempted to explore – and which offer privacy – are vital. **Hedges** are useful, and taller **banks of perennials** that screen smaller kinds from view will add atmosphere. **Evergreens** will maintain form and structure all year round, but avoid over-using them or the effect can become oppressive.

LILIES

Plant lily bulbs in February or March and, depending on the variety, they can be flowering any time from late spring to early autumn. The huge trumpet flowers look exotic, and many kinds are strongly fragrant. Choose a spot where the bulbs are in the shade of low surrounding plants but the flower stems can grow out into the sun. Lilies like well-drained ground, so the bulbs aren't left sitting in saturated soil where they might rot, but the soil must retain moisture. Help create these conditions by incorporating plenty of well-rotted organic matter such as garden compost, leafmould or old manure. Many lilies need lime-free soil so check the small print on the label before buying.

Most lilies need to be very deeply planted (around 2½ times the depth of the bulb when measured from nose to tip), and since they're big bulbs this can mean making a planting hole 20cm (8in) or more deep. Once planted, they can be left in the same place – they do best undisturbed until they badly need digging up and dividing, which may not be for several years.

If your garden soil isn't suitable, lilies will do well in large tubs or troughs filled with potting compost. For lime-hating species, look for the special lime-free version of John Innes compost (described on the bag as 'ericaceous'), or use peat-free ericaceous compost, and repot them into fresh compost every year in early spring. Good lilies for growing in containers are generally those with short, strong stems – garden centres and specialist bulb catalogues mark suitable varieties.

CREATIVE CONTAINERS

Use pots of plants positioned at different heights to create tiered planting schemes. If the garden is on a natural slope, turn it into a stepped terrace, which provides plenty of opportunities to experiment with glamorous potted displays. Otherwise make full use of steps, shelves and tables or even an old plank stood on bricks or breeze blocks to 'stage' a display. Banking up colourful displays round the edges of a small garden helps to accentuate the cosy feeling of enclosure.

Growing as much as possible in pots gives you enormous versatility in a small space as you can move things round at will, and rearrange the same 'core collection' of all-year-round plants to make fresh new displays. You can also ring the changes by bringing in exciting annuals for a single season, or put together a striking summer show using exotics that need winter protection.

Take advantage of new, innovative types of containers to increase the floral potential of a small patch. There are containers that strap around drainpipes (so even your plumbing looks showy) and you can find natty gadgets that enable you to hook up several ordinary pots or plastic towers with planting pockets all the way up. There are also plastic pouches that hang up against a wall – they're intended for semi-trailing summer bedding, such as lobelia and verbena, and create a solid waterfall of bloom once the plants have grown together.

CONTAINER CHOICES

Today there's a huge range of containers to choose from, made from all sorts of materials.

Plastic is the cheapest and very lightweight. It's not always the prettiest to look at, but since it's not porous it means compost holds moisture well. If you use trailing plants around the front edges of the container you can't really see what it's made of.

Ceramic containers also retain moisture well. Their shiny surfaces in a good range of colours make great contrasts with plant material.

Wooden tubs and planters look traditional, and they stand up well to cold weather so are often used for all-year-round plants such as camellias. They can be painted (traditional square Versailles tubs are usually painted white or dark green) or left as natural wood (half barrels are popular). It's difficult to treat them since a lot of preservatives can affect plants, and even so they'll rot in time, but for 10 years or so they look great.

Shiny metal containers or florists' buckets are fashionable for contemporary gardens. They are expensive, but durable, although need buffing up to keep them looking clean and shiny (they soon show up soil splashes). They are cold inside in winter, so best used for summer displays, and are very fashionable for growing salads or veggies in. Just make sure they are equipped with drainage holes in the base (drill them yourself if necessary).

Clay pots made of plain or slightly patterned terracotta look natural and show plants off perfectly. They are porous, so keep roots cool, but also lose a lot of moisture through their sides so need slightly more watering than plastic pots. Some are described as 'frost-proof', which means the container is made of good-quality materials that should withstand being left outside in winter without cracking or shattering. It doesn't mean the pot will protect tender plants from winter cold.

USE HANGING BASKETS FOR PRIVACY

A wide-open skyline allows outsiders to overlook your garden from windows of nearby buildings, but hanging baskets can create a crafty solution. Use pergola poles to create an overhead 'gantry' from which to suspend a screen of hanging baskets that form a floral canopy and give the area more privacy. Increase the 'blocking out' effect by fixing planted plastic sleeves high up on the upright support poles. Use reliable and free-flowering summer bedding plants (particularly geraniums, blue lobelia and petunias), which are well known for pumping out flowers continuously from planting time at the end of May until cold weather brings their display to an end in October.

Various kinds of hanging baskets are available. Natural seagrass or twiggy 'nests' look very green but have quite a short lifespan since they rot easily. They also need lining to stop compost trickling out through the gaps – use fibre liners or a circle cut from an old woolly jumper to line a wire basket. Plastic bowl-shaped baskets hold moisture much better, and incorporate a fitted drip tray in the base so water doesn't splash out and make a mess on the paving underneath. People don't find them as attractive as more traditional styles, but once plants trail down over the sides they hide the plastic.

If hanging baskets are within easy reach of the street, keep them safe by fitting an anti-theft device – a small padlock securing the basket chain to its hook or bracket is all that's needed.

♣ The secret of good hanging baskets lies in generous watering (twice daily in really hot weather) and weekly feeding in summer. Let them dry out and the display will come to a premature end.

EASY WATERING

Since hanging baskets, window boxes and tiered displays of pots are often difficult to reach when watering, install an automatic watering system run by a timer. Besides simplifying routine watering in summer, it's also useful if you are very busy, away from home a lot or want to take a summer holiday, since you don't need to ask someone to do the watering for you.

The type of system that's best for watering pots uses small-bore pipes with nozzles at the end of thin 'spaghetti tubes' that drip individually into each pot. You can buy the bits as a kit to assemble yourself to suit your own layout (find them at larger garden centres or via the Internet – you can also buy extra bits to add on to extend the layout). The black pipes are easily hidden behind pergola poles, etc., so you don't see the 'plumbing'. When installed for watering at ground level they can be covered with gravel or tucked behind troughs.

Set the timer, which fits onto an outdoor tap that's left 'on', to water plants several times a day for a few minutes each time. Be prepared to vary the settings depending on the state of the weather, the size of the plants and how fast they are growing. If you don't need a system that switches itself on and off, you can leave out the water timer and simply turn the tap on and off manually whenever you want to do the watering – it's still far quicker and easier than going round with a hose or watering can yourself.

The most effective times to water plants are early in the morning and in the evening when conditions are cool. This means plants can take up water instead of losing half of it to evaporation, so it's quite 'green' and saves money if you are on metered water. Leave an irrigation system in place from spring to autumn – in winter it's safest to gather all the tubing up and store it under cover, since it may start to leak if water inside it freezes solid. Rodents, including squirrels, often nibble holes in the plastic, too – it sounds strange but it's true!

Grow dried flower confetti

Dried flower petals are very popular as natural confetti and for all sorts of hand-made crafts. Some petals are grown commercially and sold in packets at hobby centres, craft markets and some florists, but it's very easy to do your own at home if you grow the right sort of flowers – delphiniums, larkspur, cornflower, calendula marigold, pinks, white marguerite daisy, rose, viola and pansy are best. No kilns, ovens or heaters are needed – the petals are air dried, naturally.

Delphiniums are one of the most popular flowers for producing dried petals, but use the same technique for drying other kinds of petals too.

1. Delphinium flowers are ready to pick when the bottom flower on the spike is just starting to produce seedpods (with flowers such as calendula marigold, wait until the flower is fully open, just before it would start to shed petals naturally).

2. Cut the whole flower spike and stand it in a container of water placed on a sheet of clean, dry newspaper. Choose a room with plenty of air circulation.

3. Allow the petals to fall onto the table as the blooms go over (this can take around 10 days). Leave them where they fall and just let them dry very slowly. This way they keep their shape and colour.

4. When completely dry, gather the petals up and store in the dark (so the petals don't fade) in an airtight jar with a sachet of silica gel crystals. Store the sachets in a warm, dry place such as the airing cupboard for several weeks beforehand so they are completely dry to start with. The same sachets can be reused indefinitely by re-dehydrating them in this way between uses.

5. Use the dry petals as flower confetti or for sprinkling on a table as decoration. They can also be used for decorating candles (see page 175).

Landscape around a hot tub

A hot tub is the ultimate luxurious 'extra' for a secret garden, allowing you to discover your inner Tarzan and Jane. Create sumptuous surroundings to make the most of a hot tub when you're inside it looking out, and to disguise the plumbing and rather tank-like exterior when you're outside looking in. A lush, tropical-style planting scheme helps to give the area around a hot tub an exclusive spa-like feeling. Use plants that will enjoy the humid environment and won't shed annoying leaves into the water.

1. In the space around the tub plant a tree fern, which creates a light, lacy canopy of fronds overhead. Alternatively, go for a false castor oil plant (*Fatsia japonica*) that, despite its exotic large-leafy looks, is actually as tough as old boots. Hardy banana (*Musa basjoo*) is also very effective, and survives outside in all but the very hardest winters. Just stand a good-sized plant (still in its garden centre pot) inside a classy ceramic pot for instant good looks. It's then easy to move or replace if you fancy a change of scene. Use evergreens to keep the area fully clothed all year round, since you can use a hot tub outside in even the worst of weathers. But for obvious reasons, avoid anything prickly. (fig. 1)

2. Create a showy curtain of tropical-looking plants grown in hanging baskets for the summer. Suspended at different levels they'll help create an enclosed feeling even when you can see through the plants slightly. Pendulous begonias and New Guinea busy lizzies make a colourful combination that smacks of the Amazon rain forest. Both are cold-tender, so store begonia corms indoors over winter, and take cuttings of busy lizzies to keep on the windowsill till next summer. (fig. 2)

3. To make even more of a display, add tubs of exotic looking flowers such as African lily (hardy agapanthus), ginger lilies (*Hedychium*), canna and pink arum lilies – the latter three grow from tubers that need storing indoors in winter, but they don't take up anywhere like as much room as a full-grown plant. Tubs of hardy garden lilies are also very exotic looking (see the growing guide on page 166). (fig. 3)

4. Position free-standing outdoor furniture round the hot tub to help disguise it and help the straight, solid and often brightly coloured sides blend into the garden. Use rather squarish outdoor armchairs, or an outdoor sofa, pushed back against the garden walls and the sides of the hot tub to make an inviting 'conversation pit' for pre- or post-hot-tub relaxation. Use furniture that's safe to be left outside all year round, so it forms part of the design of the area. All-weather wicker looks like rattan furniture but its made of plastic so it's fine left out full time. Make sure any cushions are damp-proof, as you're sure to sit down before you're perfectly dry after a spa session. (fig. 4)

FIG. I

FIG. 2

FIG. 3

FIG. 4

MAKE THE MOST OF A SECRET GARDEN – TRANSFORM A BASEMENT WELL

A good many basement flats have sunken, odd-shaped areas outside their doors and windows – these are often little more than a rabbit-warren of dark, damp and dingy gaps between buildings that do nothing except accumulate leaves and litter. But with a bit of thought, they can be transformed into a mini rainforest, which greatly enhances the views from the windows and creates a sensation of spaciousness.

There's normally little or no bare soil in this situation, so create a lush tropical-looking garden in containers. To make best use of very limited space, use a mixture of tubs and troughs, in several different sizes, and add hanging baskets if there's room. Don't use real exotic plants, as there'll be no room to give them winter protection. Cheat instead and use plants that are hardy or nearly-so, but just look lush and tropical, and enjoy shade and shelter. Good plants include Japanese maple, camellia, Solomon's seal and hardy ferns. For summer flowers go for dusky cranesbill and astrantia – both are shade-tolerant perennials that can stay put for several years. If you want summer bedding plants for a bigger jolt of colour, then fuchsias and petunias will do best as they flower in light shade.

Find room for one large 'star plant' to act as a centrepiece and give the garden instant gravitas – a tall tree fern that stands up above a display of smaller plants creates a dramatic lacy 'umbrella' overhead.

But be warned, it will be pricy. Disguise drainpipes on surrounding walls, standing a tree fern in front, or using special pots that clip on.

Another trick is to box in drainpipes by wiring narrow sections of trellis in place (choose white plastic trellis as it lasts well in damp conditions and reflects light) and covering them with a climber. Annual climbers are fine but choose ones that don't need full-time bright sunlight – purple bell vine (*Rhodochiton*) looks good with dangling purplish tubular bells. For a permanent climber choose a clematis – again pick one that's happy in not-too-much light and won't grow too big. *Clematis* x *triternata* 'Rubromarginata' is good – it has masses of small, white cross-shaped flowers with mauve tips to the narrow petals, and unusually they are strongly scented. In the enclosed humid environment the scent will hang on the air, and be more noticeable than usual.

Decorate candles with dried petals

Any kind of candle can be used, plain or coloured, but for best effect use plump, white, church-style ones. Home-made floral candles make good gifts for friends, or use them as centrepieces in dinner-table decorations for special occasions. As a final flourish, sprinkle matching flower petal confetti all around on the table.

1. Pour boiling water into a heatproof oven dish and dip one side of the candle in it briefly, to soften a thin outer layer of wax.

2. Roll the semi-melted section of candle immediately over a light sprinkling of dry flowers and bits of dried herb laid out flat on a board. They'll stick in place, but the wax only stays sufficiently melted for a few seconds, so work quickly.

3. Repeat, working on a different section of candle each time until all the outside is decorated. You don't want a solid layer of flowers, just a very light, even sprinkling dotted over the outside of the candle.

CHAPTER 12
THE COTTAGE GARDEN

Centuries ago, most people lived and worked out in the countryside, and relied on their pocket-hanky-sized garden to fill their larder. Today cottage gardens are romantic, flower-filled creations that lots of folk aspire to when they retire or 'down-size' to create their rural idyll. But why wait? You don't need a thatched country cottage in a quaint chocolate-box village – this type of garden uses space so effectively it makes a good template for any small plot, so even if you live in the city you can enjoy homely, cottage-garden charm.

Cottage gardens are what many folk dream of. Using plants with that relaxed 'cottagey' feel is key – and there is no shortage of choice. Artefacts, too, will bring a taste of cottage life, and vegetables and fruits among the flowers are essential.

WHAT MAKES A COTTAGE GARDEN?

Roses around the door, a white picket fence and a garden that's overflowing with a riotous jumble of flowers; that's the classic cottage garden. Flowers spill out of the borders over the edges of the lawn, every tiny space is crammed with quirky rustic knick-knacks, there are no straight lines and it's all so packed with plants that you can't see any bare soil – even the gravel paths are colonised by self-sown plants. Vegetables, fruit and herbs mingle with the flowers, and the whole garden is alive with butterflies, bees and other beneficial insects busy 'working' the blooms. The effect is wonderfully natural and romantic, redolent of a bygone age. But it's not due to ancient wisdom – behind the apparent chaos there's a little underlying order.

A cottage garden is great for anyone who enjoys tinkering and hates throwing things away. It's also brilliant for plant lovers, with bags of scope for propagating your own plants and incorporating 'finds' from plant fairs or bits and pieces swapped with friends. Cheap and cheery, do-it-yourself, make-do-and-mend – cottage gardeners are natural recyclers. It's a perfect style of garden for a recession.

GET THE LOOK

THE DESIGN

A cottage garden isn't for the control-freak, or the sort of person who likes everything in its proper place – nor is it a designer's dream. Most cottage gardens 'evolve' over a period of time, usually from whatever people inherited when they bought the house. The trick is to throw away the rulebook, and let nature lend a hand.

Allow lawns to 'shrink' as you enlarge borders little by little to make more room for plants, and make rustic paths wherever people need to walk, by spreading gravel or sinking bricks into the soil. Cottage-garden paths are often far narrower than is usually recommended, and can be uneven. It's no bad thing and, even though you may not be able to push a wheelbarrow around, it slows you down so you can't help taking your time to admire the flowers and watch the garden wildlife.

Create borders with gentle curves, and fill them with exuberant flowers – plants can safely be shoe-horned in at far greater density than the 'proper' spacing. Add recycled bits and pieces as ornaments in any space that isn't otherwise occupied. By normal standards there are far too many 'ingredients', and by rights it should look a mess, but somehow it doesn't. The secret lies in how it's all put together.

Top tip: easy care

For a low-maintenance cottage-garden border, omit plants that need special attention or regular digging up and dividing. Concentrate solely on annual self-seeders and strong perennial spreaders – they'll fight it out amongst themselves, with the fittest surviving and smothering out any weeds.

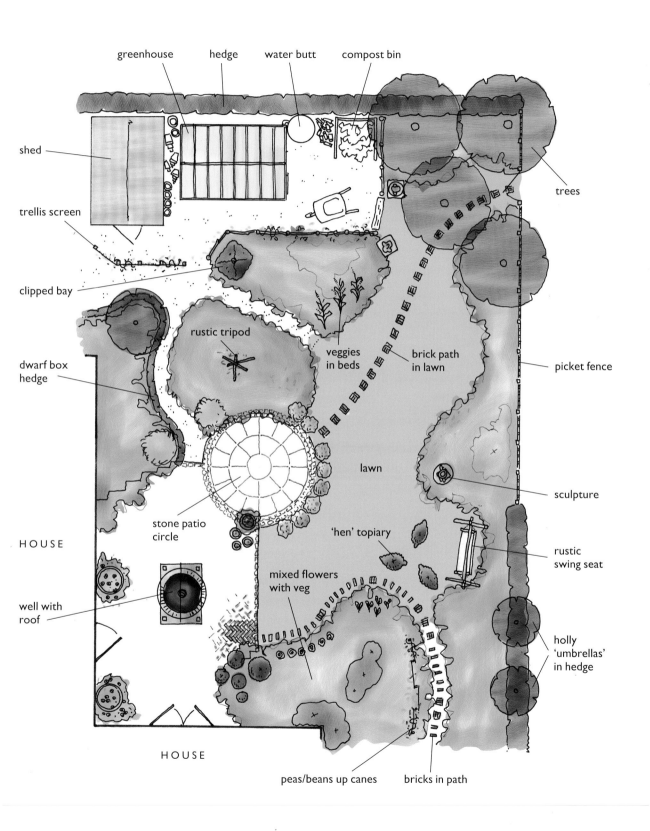

greenhouse

hedge

water butt

compost bin

shed

trellis screen

clipped bay

trees

rustic tripod

dwarf box
hedge

veggies
in beds

brick path
in lawn

picket fence

stone patio
circle

lawn

sculpture

'hen' topiary

rustic
swing seat

well with
roof

mixed flowers
with veg

holly
'umbrellas'
in hedge

HOUSE

HOUSE

peas/beans up canes

bricks in path

THE PLANTS

Cottage gardens are all about **romantic flowers**, and the more the merrier. Contrary to popular belief they don't have to be genuine old-fashioned flowers (which are now often hard-to-come-by collectors kinds, and not the easiest to cultivate). To create a classic cottage-garden look, go for the more **traditional country flowers** such as delphiniums, lupins, clematis, roses, foxgloves, campanula, phlox and anything with daisy flowers – combine these with more modern 'surprises' such as ornamental grasses. A sprinkling of the prettier **wildflowers** such as ox-eye daisies, primroses and cowslips are also a 'must'.

The trick of using plants successfully lies in creating a series of little **cameo floral combinations** of perhaps two or three plants – they should complement each other colour-wise and have contrasting shapes. To create a whole border, make up several combinations and add them together, then keep going till you've filled all the space. Good pairings include penstemon and lavender, hardy cranesbills and astilbes, sea holly with campanula, foxgloves with white willow herb and tulips with wallflowers.

People think of cottage gardens as a riotous jumble of random colours, but in practice mixing everything together can just look a frightful mess. It's far easier to limit yourself to a **small colour scheme** based around pink, mauve and purple, or yellow, white and grey – this gives a busy border a sense of order. You'll hear people say flowers never clash, although most agree that orange and pink rarely work together.

Cottage gardens are traditionally summer gardens, with very little out-of-season interest. To combat this, underplant borders with carpets of naturalised **spring bulbs** starting from snowdrops, followed by daffodils and finishing with early summer alliums (ornamental onions) and Dutch iris. Add extra interest by using tubs planted with tulips, polyanthus or double daisies for spring colour.

In winter you are reliant on evergreens, but use them sparingly or the effect won't be very cottagey. **Dwarf box hedging** gives year-round outline to garden paths, or use a cluster of box balls in different sizes as a punctuation mark at the end of a busy flower border. Use box balls on short stalks to echo the same shapes elsewhere. Clip bay into a formal pyramid shape to contrast with informal flowers all around (it also helps to control the plant) and use the leaves you snip off for cooking. Clipped holly also makes good topiary; perhaps have a small umbrella-shaped tree growing up above the line of a hedge. Use **a topiary family of hen and chicks** in the lawn, or grow a few potted topiary shapes to dot around wherever they are needed (they are useful for filling temporary gaps in a flower border when something has died down early in summer).

Use **ivies** imaginatively – they look stunning grown across the risers of a short flight of garden steps and kept closely clipped, or grow them as year-round evergreens in hanging basket displays. And don't stick to plain green evergreens – gold, purple or variegated forms can look stunning and in summer they make brilliant backdrops for flowers.

Cottage plant supports

Make your own rustic trellis by fixing lengths of straight hazel (sold for use as bean poles) together. Tie the junctions with tarred twine to hold them firmly without using nails. Alternatively, bend long, straight willow 'withies' over to make a very natural-looking arch or tunnel, again tying the cross-over points. Don't worry if it looks a tad irregular and uneven – it's meant to be rustic – the more higgledy-piggledy the better.

Use home-made plant frames (or simply push twiggy sticks in the ground) to support over-floppy perennials (though in a busy cottage-garden border neighbouring plants usually hold each other up as they are so close together).

Add height to a busy border by using rustic timber tripods instead of formal obelisks (see page 184). These make good places to grow traditional cottage-garden favourites such as clematis, pillar roses, honeysuckle or sweet peas. The supports themselves create contrasts of shape, size and colour with all the surrounding plants, which visually breaks up large areas of contrasting colours, making it easier to take in.

Make a rustic tripod

These tripods are easy to make, and you don't have to be too fussy – a tumbledown finish will add instant vintage charm that people pay a fortune for in posh designer shops. Use natural unpainted wooden tree stakes, as they've been treated to withstand life outdoors and they come with one pointed end so it's easy to hammer them into the ground. If you've pruned your own trees you might find a few straight-ish bits of branch you can cut to length. They won't last as long as bought timber, which has been treated, but who cares when the end result is free and you can easily knock up a replacement?

1. Take three posts of different lengths (between 1–2m/3–6ft) and hammer them into the ground to make a tripod. (fig. 1)

2. Measure the distance between the uprights, and cut several cross pieces to length. Screw the cross pieces to the uprights to complete the tripods – they don't have to be placed at regular intervals. To make it easier, screw the screws right through the first piece of timber before you attach the cross pieces. (fig. 2)

3. Plant a climber to train over the tripod. Plant it inside the tripod to avoid the risk of yanking it out of the ground. (fig. 3)

4. Spread the stems out evenly all round the structure and tie them in place with soft string. Spiral the stems around the tripod so you 'concertina' the greatest length of stem into the least space, for maximum flower power. (fig. 4)

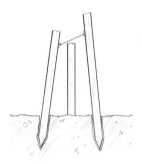

FIG. 1

FIG. 2

FIG. 3

FIG. 4

RECYCLED ORNAMENTS

All sorts of household items can be recycled to use in the garden as decorations, as can inexpensive 'finds' from jumble sales, junk shops and boot fairs. They'll help turn a patch of flowers into a personalised paradise full of unique and inspirational art 'objects'. With a little flair, almost anything can be reborn as a rustic garden feature.

An old ceramic sink makes a great little water feature, with a traditional hand pump as a 'tap' and circulating pump underneath so it keeps running. Alternatively, coat the outside of a sink with a home-made fake stone cladding (see top tip, page 186) to turn the container into a garden for growing alpines. Look for old cracked or chipped kitchen bowls, metal basins, a kettle that's lost its lid, or an old metal flour bin to turn into rustic plant containers. Since they'll only contain a small amount of compost, use them to grow plants like sedums or houseleeks that don't need much soil and don't mind drying out. The finished results can be placed in all sorts of odd gaps round the garden, or stood on tables, stone blocks or flat-topped bits of tree stump.

Old chimney pots make great garden ornaments – put them at the junction of a path or make them the centrepiece of a little 'garden within a garden'. There's no need to fill the entire chimney with compost, use the hollow centre to store a stack of plastic flower pots stood the wrong way, then sit one the right way up on top of the stack to hold some plants. You can use any mixture of summer annuals – for a traditional, cottage-garden look go for old favourites such as lobelia, fuchsia and pelargonium. Or be more adventurous and mix blue fescue grass with blue-flowered convolvulus. Alternatively, use houseleeks, which won't need so much watering. Pack the pot full of plants to give an instant effect, and water well to settle them in.

Make a hibernating hotel

A busy cottage garden, or a patch of wildflower meadow, is a natural haven for insects in summer (unknown to the owners, the average garden hosts up to 2,000 different insect species), but in winter they need somewhere safe to escape from the cold weather. Other garden wildlife, such as frogs, toads, newts and hedgehogs, also appreciate a winter retreat where they can hibernate. It's also good policy to leave a few logs in the garden or let piles of dry dead leaves build up in the bottom of a hedge. Alternatively, for a novel garden feature with wildlife appeal, why not make a hibernating hotel?

1. Take a few old pallets or veg boxes made of thin wooden slats (which your greengrocer may be glad to get rid of), and stack them up in a wild corner that won't be disturbed. Nail them together if need be, so they don't fall over if a fox or cat tries to climb on them.

2. Stuff a selection of different materials into the gaps to create pockets with gaps of varying sizes to suit different 'lodgers'. Slates, tiles and flattish stones make nooks and crannies for newts and frogs. For insects cram some gaps with rolled up bits of corrugated cardboard in a plastic tube, so the ends are accessible but the sides are waterproofed. Pack other gaps with fir cones and bundles of canes and sticks for lacewings and other insects.

3. Pretty it all up by pushing pots of evergreen herbs or rock plants in on their sides so the foliage spills out round the edges. Besides creating lots of 'vacancies', the result can look surprisingly good in the garden.

Top tip: Fake stone cladding

Mix sand, cement and peat-free multipurpose plant compost to create a fake cladding for coating old containers (old sinks are ideal). Coat the container with a bonding agent and, when this is tacky, plaster on the mixture. Allow three weeks for it to dry properly.

Create a dual-purpose cottage-garden bed

In the past, cottage gardens traditionally mixed flowers, fruit, veg, salads and herbs in the same bed to save space. Today you'll probably produce more edible crops from a separate kitchen garden area, where it is easier to keep them safe from slugs and other pests. It's still fun to recreate the olde-worlde charm of a traditional mixed cottage-garden bed, however, and if you choose crops with care you can still collect a useful harvest.

Choose an area that's easily accessible from the house, with a hard path made of gravel, brick or stone around it so you can go out to pick food at any time of year without having to pull on wellies. It should be in a fairly sunny spot with good soil (work in plenty of well-rotted organic matter and choose your plants to include a mixture of decorative and useful edible plants).

A good rule of thumb for planting a border is 'tallest at the back, shortest at the front', but make a bed seem less predictable by moving a few taller plants forward to make irregular lines. This divides the border up into a series of smaller 'planting bays' that make it easier on the eye, and also creates little surprises that you only see as you walk past.

1. Make a background of decorative-but-edible shrubs such as purple-leaved filbert for nuts, a 'John Downie' crab-apple tree (the best variety for making crab-apple jelly) or a standard gooseberry bush on a 1m (3ft) high stem. Alternatively, use cordon apple trees as a fruiting screen. If there's a wall at the back, use it for growing a fan-trained fruit tree. The morello cherry (the cooking sort) grows well on a north-facing wall. Use a south- or west-facing wall for peaches, apricots, nectarines or plump, meltingly juicy 'Doyenne du Comice' pears.

2. For flowers, use artichoke (large, silvery, architectural leaves and big knobbly silver-green and purple edible flowerheads), purple fennel (feathery purple foliage topped with yellow cow-parsley-like flowers) and bellflowers (*Campanula sp.*). If there's room, include other flowers for cutting such as dahlias, zinnia or sweet peas. In a real old cottage garden these would have formed a valuable cash crop, sold at the garden gate with an honesty box for collecting the money. Keep closely to your colour scheme where possible (here it's largely purple and yellow.)

3. Edge the path with a low fringe of purplish-red frilly lettuce, parsley and chives (which has edible purple flowers). Add violas or pansies, which are also edible and good for pressing for greetings cards and bookmarks.

4. Stand all the plants in place to see how they look together so you can make any last-minute alterations before planting them properly.

5. As a finishing touch, add a few miniature woven hazel or willow hurdles to the edge of the path to hold the plants back. Although it's lovely to see flowers spilling over the edges, they can sometimes get in the way of a very narrow cottage-garden path. The contrasting twiggy border adds an instant, vintage, time-worn style.

MAKE THE MOST OF A COTTAGE GARDEN – GROW FOOD FOR FREE

In the past, country people ate all sorts of foods they found growing wild in the countryside – today it's known as 'foraging' and is becoming quite fashionable in foodie circles. To collect real wild food you need the landowner's permission, and it's not advisable to collect from roadside verges due to traffic dust, petrol fumes and the risk that chemicals may have been sprayed. But without going to any trouble you can make use of wild produce that grows in your garden. All sorts of unlikely-sounding weeds make good eating, when you know what to do with them.

For a wild salad use the soft young tips of chickweed, young leaves of jack-by-the-hedge (garlic-tasting) and a touch of hairy bittercress (a good watercress substitute). Dandelion (use the young central leaves after blanching them under a bucket for several days first) and young leafy shoots of hawthorn (once called bread-and-cheese by country people) are also tasty. Some salad leaves grown in gardens today were originally wild plants in this country – common sorrel, lamb's lettuce (aka corn salad), watercress and miner's lettuce (aka spring beauty, *Claytonia perfoliata*) are all available to grow from seed from some commercial seed firms. They also grow well in containers.

For a green vegetable to accompany a meal, use young fat-hen leaves, young ground elder leaves or nettle tops as spinach substitutes – stir fry briefly in a knob of butter till tender, (usually they only need a few minutes) then chop finely.

WEED RISOTTO
SERVES: 4

Preparation time
40 minutes

Ingredients
A handful of young ground
   elder leaves
A handful of nettle tops
Olive oil
1 onion, chopped
1 clove of garlic, chopped
Splash if white wine
1 cup of risotto rice
700ml of hot chicken stock
2 tablespoons of grated
   Parmesan cheese
Knob of butter

Method

1. Wash the elder leaves and nettle tops to remove dust or bugs. Blanch them by placing them in a saucepan and pouring enough boiling water over to cover. Leave for a minute or so, then stop them cooking any more by plunging them into cold water for another minute or so. Set them aside in a colander to drain.

2. Heat a glug of olive oil in a strong skillet and gently fry the onion and garlic. When they are soft, add a splash of white wine and stir in the rice.

3. As the wine is absorbed, add the hot chicken stock a little at a time with a ladle and keep stirring constantly to stop it sticking.

4. When the rice is completely cooked, but the risotto is still slightly runny (after about 20 minutes), stir in the cheese and a good knob of butter. Lastly, add the blanched weeds. Serve with warm crusty bread.

INDEX